Another Chance

Another Chance
Learning to Like Yourself

Cecil Murphey

The Westminster Press
Philadelphia

Unless otherwise identified, scripture quotations are from the Revised Standard Version of the Bible, copyrighted 1946, 1952, © 1971, 1973 by the Division of Christian Education of the National Council of the Churches of Christ in the U.S.A., and are used by permission.

Quotations marked NIV are taken from the *Holy Bible: New International Version.* Copyright © 1978 by the New York International Bible Society. Used by permission of Zondervan Bible Publishers.

Quotations marked TLB are taken from *The Living Bible,* copyright 1971 by Tyndale House Publishers, Wheaton, Ill. Used by permission.

The quotation from *Necessary Losses,* pp. 325–326, by Judith Viorst, copyrighted 1986, is used by permission of Simon & Schuster.

For the protection and privacy of the individuals involved, names and minor details in citing examples in this book have been changed.

Book design by Gene Harris

First edition

Published by The Westminster Press®

Philadelphia, Pennsylvania

PRINTED IN THE UNITED STATES OF AMERICA

9 8 7 6 5 4 3 2 1   3·88

Library of Congress Cataloging-in-Publication Data

Murphey, Cecil B.
    Another chance.

    1. Self-respect—Religious aspects—Christianity.
I. Title.
BV4647.S43M87   1987   248.8′6   87–10517
ISBN 0–664–24093–3 (pbk.)

I want to express my appreciation to Vernon R. Gramling, a pastoral counselor in Atlanta, for the insights afforded to me, first through a lecture and then in personal discussions. His comments have been helpful to me in the development of this book.

Contents

1

The Question
of Self-Worth

Donna, a gifted clinical psychologist, holds a PhD and has successfully practiced for eighteen years. She headed the psychological testing program of a state university for six years and has been in private practice for twelve. Donna is now forty years old.

"I look at what I've done and where I've been and I ask, Has it been worth it? What is my self-worth? If my meaning comes from these achievements and activities, what happens when I don't do them anymore? Do I have any value left?"

Jeremy received a report from his doctor on his sixty-seventh birthday. "What a birthday present," he said. "You hand me a death sentence."

The diagnosis was cancer. The lab report and the doctor's explanation carefully avoided answering Jeremy's question, "How long do I have?" Yet Jeremy could not drop the question. In fact, it raised many more: Who am I? Is this all there is? What happens after I'm gone? Why does it have to be me? Look at what I can't do anymore. Is this the end for me? If there is any meaning in life, where is it now?

When Margie's husband died, she set herself one goal: to raise her two boys to the best of her ability. The elder graduated from college and immediately went into a high-paying position. The younger, in his second year of college 3,000 miles away, received a full scholarship. Both boys have since married and have their own families.

"I don't know what to do with myself now," Margie said. "My whole world revolved around my sons. They don't need me anymore. Nobody needs me." She is understandably depressed.

Bruce, a pastor with twenty-one years of experience, left the parish. "I had to find myself," he said. The record shows he was a hard worker. In all three of his pastorates, he started with an average weekly worship attendance of under one hundred. Within five years, each of the congregations had at least doubled. He carried on an extensive counseling schedule, along with a heavy involvement in social programs.

"People came to me for help. Why did they come? Only because I listened? I wonder if they ever saw me as a human being. Would I have any value if I didn't give, give, give? Did any of them like me for being me?" He shook his head. "Anybody like me, who gives himself to people, gets love, affection, respect in return. I had to get away from my role to find out that I was more than the functions I filled."

Different people. Differing circumstances. Yet the questions sound remarkably similar. They each ask, in their individual way, What am I worth now that I'm not who I used to be?

These men and women don't base their questions on how others view their abilities or attainments. These questions of self-value are prompted by their feelings about themselves. Such feelings are encountered at various stages of life, sometimes more than once.

A simplistic response to these people would be to say that they lack self-love. If they had always been loved and always known they were loved, they would not find the present situation so traumatic. They would have a high level of self-esteem and self-love to sustain them. Because they didn't always perceive they were loved (and perhaps they were not), they started off at an emotional disadvantage.

But isn't that true for all of us? Have any of us *always* felt loved? Most people probably would not say, "I never in my life—not once—ever felt loved"; they would affirm that they think well of themselves, although with some qualification.

"I like myself, but . . ."

"I feel good about myself part of the time (or most of the time), but . . ."

For most of us, the experience of being loved is a sometime thing. As a therapist friend says, "None of us gets enough loving. We all lack somewhere in loving ourselves. What we didn't get in infancy, we have to look for elsewhere."

This book will offer some suggestions about where to look for this love. The exercises in the chapters and in the Appendixes will also help you in your quest. Insights credited to Vern are from Vern Gramling.

The Question of Self-Esteem

Self-esteem involves our personal assessment of who we are. This self-perception guides our thoughts, feelings, and actions toward life. Self-perception predisposes us to respond to events either negatively or positively. When we talk about our sense of self-esteem, it's as if we stood across the room and looked objectively at ourselves. However, what we consider objective is actually the most personalized, subjective assessment possible.

Our sense of self-esteem is based not only on our perception of who we are but also on how we feel about who we are. Self-worth is based on our evaluation of material from two perspectives.

First, we compare ourselves to other people, especially the significant others in our lives. If these people constantly tell us "You're wonderful!" they may actually be setting impossible standards for us. Their words may also have a reverse effect. Because we know that no one is good and wonderful and brilliant all the time, we may question the truthfulness of such overwhelmingly positive remarks and suspect the worst.

Sometimes people may say the right words but their gestures and body language convey a different message. When this happens, most of us instinctively believe the body language and dismiss the words.

We also perceive ourselves in comparison to what we feel we would like to be or who we feel we ought to be. Our ideal self, the person we want to be, represents the internalization of the values transmitted by culture, by experience, and by the significant people in our lives. This also explains why we all have differences in our ideal selves. Every culture and subculture holds up different qualities to emulate or to shun.

We measure our self-esteem by the discrepancy between how we perceive ourselves and our ideal selves. The smaller the discrepancy, the higher our self-esteem.

In our search for the ideal, many of us in the church focus on Jesus Christ or the apostle Paul or one of the Old Testament saints. When we compare ourselves with this ideal, we readily see our own shortcomings and inadequacies. We have little sense of spiritual growth because we see only how far short we are of perfection, of reaching our ideal. Guilt hangs over us for not living up to that ideal, or we label ourselves failures for not reaching our spiritual potential.

The Question of Worth

We usually define our self-worth, value, self-esteem, self-love by what we do. In the process of change, aging, or dying, these definitions erode. Then what happens?

Old values and criteria no longer work. When we retire, have we lost our value? If we're terminally ill, does that take away our self-esteem? If we stop serving others, have we given up our purpose? If we have fulfilled our major goal in life, like Margie in raising her sons, are we now redundant?

All around us people still define themselves in the traditional ways—by their talents, looks, productivity, or possessions. Making changes, getting older, and moving toward death force many of us to reassess life. If we put our values in the wrong places, what happens now? Is it like investing our life savings in dry oil wells and ending up empty, desolate, and despairing— worthless?

What are some of the ways we invest ourselves in our search for self-worth? We may call it self-fulfillment, self-actualization, or any other term. It still comes down to a desperate, ongoing need for our life to make sense and for us to have places of value in it.

The Answer of Achievement

Suppose I make it my primary goal to become Chief Executive Officer of my company. That goal becomes number one in my life. I have less time and energy for my family and for social relationships.

I climb the corporate ladder. I finally make CEO. Then I die. Why did I put so much effort into that one achievement? Or I retire and plan a life of leisure and then learn I have cancer. I worked so hard to get to this point, and now I can't enjoy it. I had thought I knew what gave meaning to my life. Now I silently cry out, Why am I here? Is this all there is?

By contrast, we're constantly hearing about our untapped potential. One approach toward self-worth involves the now-popular view that we can do anything. "Be a no-limit person"; "You can do anything you want." We are told that nothing is impossible. As one motivational speaker frequently says, "Anything the mind can conceive and believe, it can achieve."

What happens when we fail? When we stretch for the top rung and miss? When we receive the coveted promotion, only to discover that we don't have the ability to handle it? What about our no-limit life-style then?

I once read a story about a jazz musician. A highly gifted trumpet player, he constantly tried to hit higher and richer notes. Although highly successful, he kept reaching for that impossible note—the note no one had ever played.

Finally he played before a large crowd. Improvising, as he always did, he started going up the scale, playing better than he ever had in his life. The audience felt drawn to him, mesmerized by a quality of music they'd never heard before. He reached for that final note—and failed.

The story concludes with his walking out of the theater, never to play again. He didn't want to live because he couldn't do that one thing he coveted. He believed that he was a failure, even though his competence far outshone his peers.

He put the emphasis on one thing. When that failed—and it always does ultimately—he despaired. The musician could not point to what he had achieved, only to what he could not do.

As creatures who take up space on this earth and as children of God, we have an obligation to be all we can be. We like to succeed at whatever we do. Achieving makes us proud of what we do.

Self-worth certainly has *something* to do with achievement. Yet God did not create us to measure our total value by one achievement or even by a series of achievements.

None of us accomplishes everything. We have built-in limits because of our creaturehood. Even if most of us have never pushed ourselves far enough to discover them, they exist.

Yet deep within, many of us harbor the idea, I could do it if I really decided to. Or we look back and think, I could have been the best if I had only put more effort into it. Such attitudes reveal that we still haven't come to terms with the fact that we can't do everything.

The Answer of Fame

For some, self-esteem lies in perpetuating our name. We want to become legends because of outstanding achievements, such as bravery in war or winning a political office, or by recognition of our unique talents. Yet not many of us leave monuments behind (and even those eventually corrode).

We don't have many works of art that endure. We immortalize a few artists such as Picasso, Renoir, Rembrandt, Grant Wood, or even Norman Rockwell. But we forget others who worked just as hard and never achieved the same lasting recognition.

As a writer I always hope that one of my books (or even all of them) will remain for generations to come. I'd like to have my books placed on the shelf next to Dickens, Thackeray, Hemingway, and Steinbeck. Yet reality tells me they won't be.

Most of us are ordinary people. Death leaves us without anything to take with us, and we leave little behind to be remembered by for more than a generation or two.

Vern remembers thinking, one day in high school, If I could do something great or dramatic, my name might live to the time of my great-grandchildren but probably no longer. He saw that realistically.

If our goal in life is to have people remember our names, few of us will attain that level of achievement. Some have immortalized themselves by doing it adversely. They climb a tower and shoot fifty people. They betray their country or attempt to assassinate the President. They're remembered, but their names become infamous instead of famous. These people have found that it's easier to make a hideous mark than a positive one.

Our thinking and daydreaming about achievement exposes the fallacy of what many of us have unconsciously learned. We put our energies into activities as if we expected to live forever. We work toward honing our skills and increasing our abilities. We want to yell, Look at me! See, I am of value!

The call to "look at me" reminds me of a man I've known for years. Someone described Charlie as "the guy who keeps the party alive. He's constantly the center of activity, well informed on everything from sports and politics to the latest books. He has something to contribute to every conversation. He's also the kind of man for whom they invented the word 'workaholic' during the day and maybe 'playaholic' at night. He's intense and does everything as fully and totally as he can."

But does he like himself? Does he have a high level of self-esteem? Looking at his actions, I suspect he does not. Otherwise he would not need to call attention to himself, to beg "Just look at me!"

Other Nonanswers

Owning property, expensive cars, or the newest equipment seems to make some people feel as if they have value.

Others point to their degrees from prestigious universities. One woman who works in curriculum development doesn't feel editors and writers are qualified to work with Sunday school materials unless they have gone to her alma mater, which specializes in education. I've known two classical singers who look down upon those who trained at places other than Juilliard.

If we don't have a sense of self-worth, we either fake it by pointing to something else, such as our achievements, or we walk around, head hung low, nonverbally telling the world that we have no real value.

Whether we talk about Charlie, the musician, or the people

mentioned at the beginning of this chapter, ultimately we have to face the reality that, while our activities and achievements may point out our talents, they don't give us worth.

The Question of Earning Worth

Obviously we can't make ourselves of greater worth. However, many of us fall into the trap of trying to earn our self-worth by making ourselves bigger, better, richer, stronger, healthier, more productive. If we do enough, we expect to become valuable.

We want others to accept us and fear they won't. When we fear that we are unacceptable as we are, we take that as implicit evidence that we have not yet done enough. Or we assume that our flaws and inadequacies hinder us from being loved.

For example, Charlie constantly needs to prove himself. He overworks, overplays, overtries, and probably doesn't know it. It's as if he shouts to the world, Look at this! Now am I acceptable? Did I do it right this time? Unfortunately, even if he should get a positive response to his question, he'd ask again tomorrow.

We want relationships with others. We desire intimacy and yet fear that we are not worth enough with our flaws and limitations. If we have difficulty in liking ourselves, we don't easily find acceptance by others.

Lessons from the Dying

Vern learned a lot about self-esteem and life by being around dying people in a hospice. They helped him see that the things we spend so much effort in acquiring erode when we come to the end of life. Through those experiences he found himself repeatedly asking, What makes a human being valuable?

When we hear, "You're dying," life makes a dramatic turn. We ask ourselves, What in my life has been valuable? How am I valuable?

Our Christian heritage teaches us that we are valuable because we exist. Yet we discover that we use other criteria to validate ourselves.

We have linked our worth to achievement. As death comes near we know we can no longer achieve. We have based our value on how well we filled our specific roles. Now we no longer function as parents or executives, teachers or mechanics. The process of dying strips away those roles because we can no longer maintain them.

If we live long enough, every vestige of autonomy gets stripped away. Unable to produce or achieve, we become completely dependent. How can we feel valuable in circumstances where we must turn to others even for simple body needs?

Death sounds depressing, and yet in the midst of the dying Vern discovered lessons about life. He encountered individuals who had "a certain something about them" that stood out. They had an unmistakable quality about them. They didn't deny their impending death. They held no Pollyanna-ish anticipation of better days. There was something profoundly genuine in those people, who faced their ultimate loss and still maintained a sense of self-esteem. They also retained the ability to love and to be loved.

Living in the Gap

They were learning to die well—acknowledging death while retaining faith in their self-worth. Those who die well have learned to cope successfully with the reality of helplessness. As they face their nonexistence, they accept their creatureliness. They know what they want and can't have. Those people affirm their self-worth and discover how to live "in the gap," as Vern calls it, between wanting more and accepting what they get. They retain their responsibility to become everything they can be while they face human limitations.

Most dying people want to live but will not. A few can live while dying. They live unable to have what they want most—life.

We don't find it easy to acknowledge our limits in day-to-day activities. We try to escape our limitations in many ways. We blame others for standing in our way. We bemoan our circumstances for never giving us a real chance. We work harder, believing that if we try hard enough, we can have everything we want.

We reach the end of human existence and feel empty and lonely. We didn't get the things we wanted. But we still have choices. We can abdicate from life, saying, "No matter what happens now, it doesn't matter. Life has lost all meaning."

Or we can choose the braver path. We can learn to live in the gap.

2

Never Loved?
Forever Loved?

I don't believe in a fixed level of self-esteem. While experiences in early childhood largely shape our lives, we still have choices. *We can change.*

Never Loved?

A student named Lonnie taught me one of the first conscious lessons I've ever had in the area of self-esteem.

On my first day in teaching sixth grade, I asked each pupil to read a paragraph orally. I planned to put the thirty students into five reading groups. When I called on Lonnie, he informed me that he did not read aloud because he could not and that teachers did not call upon him. "Besides that," he said, "I'm dumb."

As I stared at that small, thin boy I had my first significant insight on self-love. "How do you know you're dumb, Lonnie?" I asked.

"All my other teachers know I'm dumb. Ask them."

A few days later I visited Lonnie's house and met his mother. She said, "Just keep the kid in school until he's old enough to quit. He ain't smart enough to do much with his life anyway."

I'm sure that from his earliest days, Lonnie had heard that message again and again: "You'll never amount to anything."

I took on Lonnie as a personal challenge for the rest of the year. Every time he did something right, I praised him. I tried to make him know that I cared, and I encouraged him to try.

I assigned a bright, compassionate student to work with him.

By the end of the school year, I couldn't report a glowing success story. However, Lonnie had learned to read with some proficiency on a third-grade level. He did read aloud in his small group. I wanted to hold him back but our school policy made that difficult.

Lonnie, like any other small child, began with no clear picture of himself. He evaluated himself by using his parents as his mirror in life. As Lonnie grew older, he lived up to his perceived self-image.

What eventually happened to Lonnie? I don't know. If I accomplished anything, I did help him move from being too limited in his self-assessment. Too many other factors were working against success for Lonnie: time (trying to counteract in nine months the effects of twelve years of life), his home environment, his social atmosphere (classmates who considered him stupid), and the school system (his low grades earned him a reputation of being a slow learner).

While our environment or childhood experiences are significant, they don't make the total difference.

Forever Loved

Let me tell you about Max. He doesn't talk much about himself, and yet friends refer to him as self-assured and confident. One person put it this way: "Max exudes a spirit of I-know-who-I-am-and-I-know-what-I'm-doing. You feel comfortable around him and don't always worry about having to compliment him or say nice things to stay on his good side."

If you asked Max about his childhood, he might tell you that most of the time he knew his parents loved him. He might even say, "I've always been loved." While none of us feels loved every moment of our lives, Max has had few doubts about his being lovable.

Being loved did not give Max his self-esteem. The good parenting Max received helped him to deal more effectively with his disappointments, failures, and self-doubts. He has more resources to fall back on during those times when he feels unloved and unlovable.

All this portrays Max in a simplistic light, yet he knows who he is. He has a strong sense of self-esteem, or self-worth.

I remember two times when I observed a strong sense of self-esteem in Max. His actions themselves don't prove healthy self-esteem; people with low self-values could have done or said the same things but for different reasons. They might have tried to prove their value or used it as an opportunity to "earn" value in the eyes of others. Max acted as he did *because* of his own inner security about who he is.

Although I've known Max as a friend for years, I first met him when he was a student in a small midwestern college where I taught part-time. A nonprofit organization asked our college for donations. The dean brought pressure on students and faculty alike so that the school could report a 100 percent response. Several of us had reservations about that particular organization. We also knew the dean had a long memory about people who crossed him. When the dean came into the classroom, we dissident instructors caved in and each dropped a token dollar in the box. The students also made their contribution. All except Max.

"I'm not giving," he said when the dean shook the box in front of him.

The dean stared in disbelief and explained the importance of the event as if Max didn't know. "This is to help needy people." Max refused a second time. The dean finally asked, "Why don't you want to give? I thought you were a real Christian."

"I've decided not to give." Max smiled and turned back to his books.

At the end of the class period, I heard his friends saying they admired his stance. One of them said, "Even if I had refused, I would have felt I had to give him twenty reasons."

Max shrugged, as if surprised. "When somebody asks me for a favor or to do something I don't want to, I don't owe an explanation."

The second incident impressed me even more. Max and two classmates worked as a team on a research paper. They struggled for many hours and put in a lot of hard work.

After reading the paper, the instructor called the three students into his office. For twenty minutes he shot holes in their paper and ended by throwing it back at them. "Redo it."

I sat in the next office, separated only by a paper-thin partition. The three left the office seconds ahead of me. On my way to my next class I overheard one of them groaning about what a failure he was.

"Wait a minute," I heard Max say. "He didn't like our paper, OK? We'll do it again his way. But remember, he didn't attack *us,* only our work."

Until that time, I had never made a distinction in my own thinking between my work (of any kind) and myself. I had wrapped them both together. Max had the ability to separate criticism of the paper from criticism of himself.

The Perception

Max could have undergone the same experiences in life that Lonnie did but perceived them differently. He could have believed that his parents gave him toys as substitutes for affection. Max might have specific memories of emotional abandonment when his mother put him in bed at night and left the room while he lay in the dark and cried. He might remember when he disobeyed and heard, "You're a nasty, bad, disobedient boy" whether or not the parents actually used those words. Perception makes a great difference in our attitude of being forever loved or never loved.

Lonnie wanted to be loved (we all do) and needed to be loved. Yet I doubt that he grasped the difference between being loved for who one *is* and being loved for what one *does.*

I'm not trying to present Max and his parents as the good guys and Lonnie and his as the ones to shun. Showing their differences implies no judgment on their value as human beings. Both Max and Lonnie are equally important, whether they know it or not. The decision rests upon individual perception, not upon the events themselves.

Consider these three facts:

First, a sense of being loved has little to do with physical ability. One former pro basketball star admitted on a talk show that during an illustrious career on the courts he often asked himself, What happens when they find out I'm not any good?

Second, a sense of being loved has nothing to do with one's

physical attractiveness. I have a friend who is quite handsome. Yet when we talked about looks, he told me he has a receding chin (not true) and enormous ears (again, not true). In a discussion one day in which several of us talked honestly about our physical appearance, he said he believed he was just "barely above being called ugly." On a scale of 1 to 10, he rated himself a 3.

Third, a sense of being loved has little to do with mental ability. Extremely bright people sometimes feel stupid and, if they receive good grades in school, assume they were lucky or just worked hard. It doesn't sink in that if they were not highly intelligent all their work would make little difference.

Many high achievers look at what they have achieved, and yet, deep inside, they're convinced they are impostors and one day the company will find out and fire them.

A close friend who wrote screenplays for twenty years constantly feared that a producer or studio head would come to her one day and say, "You're fired. You're no good." Despite her recognition within the industry, she considered herself a fake.

Self-esteem does not depend on our abilities—either having them or not having them. It does not depend on achievement. *Self-esteem depends on how we view ourselves.*

Where Self-Love Begins

Our feeling of self-worth begins early in childhood. Some argue that it's established by the end of the first year, others by eighteen months. Most would agree that early childhood experiences and our perceptions of them largely determine our self-esteem. The way the significant people in our lives treat us, and the way we respond to life, profoundly affects how we view ourselves. Parents exert a powerful early influence on our self-perceptions because they condition us by the way in which they give us information about ourselves.

Negative information and experiences create a low self-image because they block the process that allows us to accept praise for our achievements. If our parents called us clumsy when we spilled milk, or lazy when we didn't want to pick up our toys, many of us naturally assumed our parents had accurately diagnosed us as clumsy or lazy. However, we were probably normal children.

A strong self-image is built on acceptance, praise, and acknowledgment of ourselves as people of value. Without positive feedback, our feelings either stay at about the same level or lessen rather than growing or enhancing our feeling of self-worth. When we don't get responses from the important people in our lives that make us feel unique and special, we tend to feel ordinary at best, normally inadequate, and useless at worst.

During those early stages of infancy we begin to assess who we are. Because of the way our mothers, fathers, and other important people in our lives relate to us, we learn about ourselves. Their words communicate their perceptions of us long before we have the ability to decide whether or not they speak with accuracy. Whatever we hear about ourselves, if we hear it often we automatically believe it. We do not have the ability to distinguish true from false.

Besides words, touching, holding, and kissing profoundly impress upon us the attitude of our parents. If they shower us with physical attention, we understand more clearly their love. When we grow up without physical affection, we infer we are not worth being loved anyway.

For example, Max knew from infancy that his parents loved him. His mother would tell him, "You are a wonderful child." She expressed her feelings frequently. She held him on her lap and read to him. He recalls she often stroked his head when she talked to him. His father never said goodbye without adding, "I love you, Max," and hugging the boy.

From the little I observed of Lonnie's home, his mother didn't mistreat him. Despite her believing he was stupid, I believe she honestly loved the boy. But she never showed her love.

We cannot blame our mothers (or others who nurture us) if we have a low sense of self-esteem. Many circumstances keep us from receiving the expressions of love we need in the beginning. Some reasons why children do not feel loved include:

- a mother who became pregnant by accident and resented her offspring
- a nurturing parent (or grandmother or older sibling) who died during the child's first two years of life
- an emotionally ill parent

- a parent who physically or emotionally abused the child
- a parent too preoccupied with other children, supporting a family as a single parent, or who pursued other interests
- a self-centered (narcissistic) parent who views the child as an extension of the parent's own self

Aside from these kinds of circumstances, normal parents may produce children who lack self-esteem. Patterns of self-love begin and receive reinforcement during the formative years. These children have never felt deeply loved. They believe they never received enough affection, time, attention, and admiration during this crucial period.

The messages of value that we need may not come from our families. We may find them somewhere else—a neighbor or a relative, a teacher who befriends us.

My friend Joan said that one special person made a tremendous difference in her life. Her alcoholic father physically abused her and, on one occasion, tried to rape her. When she was in fourth grade her pastor recognized how little love and affirmation she received at home. One day he visited her and said, "Joan, I have adopted you as my spiritual daughter. No matter what you do or where you go, I'll always love you." From then on, she spent time with his family and often called it her second home. Now thirty-eight, married, and with her own children, she told me, "Because of him, I knew I was loved. He did for me what no one else ever did."

In my own case, I came from a nondemonstrative family. Early in life, a neighborhood family let me spend a lot of time with them. I received a lot of attention there and from my elementary teachers, who made me feel important and encouraged me.

One day my fifth-grade teacher (and all-time favorite), Miss Linder, called me to her desk. She held up a paper that I had handed in, sloppily done. I will never forget what she said to me: "You're a smart boy, and you can do better work than this." She handed it back. "I want you to show me how well you can do it." I redid the paper and brought it up to her. She made me stand by the desk as she read it. Then she smiled at me and wrote the grade 100 across the top. Through the compassion of that teacher I compensated for what I did not receive (or perceive) at home.

In the beginning stages of life, we survive by our total dependence upon others. We cling to them and idealize them. We are aware only of ourselves and our connectedness to that person we later know as mother (or the one who nurtures us in her stead). As we gradually broaden our world, we learn our separateness. Our authority figures speak and act toward us, and from them we reflect who we are.

Every new bit of information we process internally changes us, for better or worse. If we learn to block out the negative forces and listen to the positive, we can change into more positive individuals.

Children's Perspective

One way that helped me see how many of us view our worth was to think about children in the church. Most of us in the Christian tradition learned "Jesus Loves the Little Children," "Jesus Loves Me," and we recall Jesus' word, "Let the children come to me" (Matt. 19:14).

As children, we lived among physically large people. They were coordinated, knowledgeable, and wise. By contrast we felt small, inadequate, and often out of place. When we entered into church membership around age twelve, what did that mean for us? (I'm not questioning here the ability of children to believe or to understand the responsibility of membership.) We still knew that the work done within the church, all the decisions made, and all the giving came from big people. Our hope lay in one day becoming physically larger and older; then we could become "real" members.

We often assumed that small meant unimportant, valueless, and therefore unlovable. The message we received as children was, "When you get big, things will be better."

It was hard enough to be small and to feel inadequate without also believing we were less valuable than adults. We were apt to conclude that our immaturity meant we were unworthy or bad.

Parents told us from time to time, "You're getting bigger and stronger. You're growing up." Despite the positive message, some of us interpreted that to imply that being small and weaker is bad.

While life seemed uncomfortable for us, our feeling of discomfort didn't make us less lovable. Some of us didn't get enough attention because we were shy, relatively inarticulate in expressing our wants, or even unaware of what we wanted. Sometimes the big people called grown-ups didn't have sensitive ears to hear us.

Even when we grow up, our sense of inadequacy doesn't go away. We want to like ourselves and to feel good about being who we are. Some of our parents used to compare us to other children—especially those who were higher achievers. When we grow up, we continue the pattern and try to establish our worth by comparing ourselves with others. We learn that life hasn't changed much. We still judge ourselves as less adequate and therefore of less value.

Vern saw this attitude among nursing students who came in to talk with him. One student made a serious error—a common experience among learners. She punished herself by insisting, "The instructors and the floor nurses don't make those errors." She said, "I feel kind of dumb. Maybe that's what's wrong with me. I'm just not smart enough." In a lengthy explanation about her mistake, she compared herself unfavorably with the more experienced teachers and floor nurses. She didn't realize that she was exactly on track for somebody of her age and inexperience.

"It's not fair to compare your inexperience with your experienced teacher," Vern explained. "If you must compare, go back to the time when she had the same level of experience that you have now."

The student didn't realize that, in order to learn, we must be able to make mistakes. However, if we berate ourselves for our mistakes, we use up valuable energy and make learning even harder. Ironically, when we have enough of a sense of self-esteem to acknowledge our mistakes, we can put our energy into correcting and learning from them. That's when we become more of who we can be, and our self-esteem grows.

Few of us feel good about ourselves when we make mistakes, especially when those around us appear to be fully competent. Our feeling of inadequacy translates into lowered self-esteem. We can't seem to grasp that we are valuable exactly where we are, even if we make mistakes and are unable to do certain things that people with more experience, time, or ability can do. We fail to realize that true self-esteem cannot be built upon the way in which we compare ourselves with others.

Comparisons with others are based upon how we see ourselves. During early stages of infancy we began to assess who we were. We learned about ourselves from the way in which our mothers, fathers, or other important people related to us. Their words communicated their perception of us long before we had the ability to judge whether or not their assessment was accurate. Whatever we heard about ourselves, we believed. Frequent repetition reinforced these ideas about ourselves, and we accepted them as true.

For example, a good friend named Don said his father constantly called him clumsy. In high school he played a good game of basketball. In college, he won a place in the marching band. Yet despite all this evidence to the contrary, down in the recesses of his psyche, Don still thought he was the most awkward person around.

Imposed Concepts

Many of us grew up hearing our parents tell us:

> "Don't be stupid!"
> "You are always so clumsy!"
> "Can't you do anything right?"
> "Why can't you be like your sister?"

If we heard such statements often enough, we absorbed them as statements of fact even if they were totally wrong.

People often spend vast amounts of time and energy in life with questions such as:

> "What's wrong with me?"
> "Why wasn't I good enough or lovable enough?"
> "Why didn't they love me?"
> "How did I let them down? I must have failed them somehow."

Finding answers to these questions, while helpful in some instances, goes beyond the scope of this book. For most of us who feel a lack of self-love, we might find it more profitable to remind ourselves:

> "I cannot undo my past."
> "I can learn to accept the present and to build on it."
> "Even if I knew why my family didn't express love, I can't do anything about it."

Instead of asking "Why?" we can proceed with the fact that some of us did not grow up with a strong sense of being loved and valued for ourselves. For us, the more profitable question becomes, "What do I do now?"

The Theological Base

Until recent years, we heard little about self-love in the church world. We heard a great deal about the negative side, which we called self-centeredness and selfishness.

There has been a new theological emphasis aimed at getting rid of "self." Had people been more precise about the terminology and more understanding of our basic need for self-love, the emphasis might not have been so destructive. Many church people spent their energy getting rid of "self," which they interpreted to include their own desires, preferences, and self-appreciation. The more they sought to "crucify self" or, as they sometimes called it, "crucify the flesh," the poorer they became spiritually. The focus on the negative produced deep guilt and a sense of failure in those who acknowledged any kind of healthy self-love.

The psychological view of self-love is that we need a significant other person in our lives to love us first. The Bible says it only slightly differently: "We love, because he first loved us" (1 John 4:19).

Our Creator God has forever loved us—even from before the formation of the world (e.g., John 3:16; Eph. 1:4). God showered love upon us without our doing anything. Ideally, during our infancy, this love and our sense of value as people comes to us through our parents. They reflect God's unconditional love for us. As they provide the nurturing experiences, we feel loved and are then enabled to love others.

God further helps us by revealing divine love to us. I became a Christian at age twenty-one. Referring to God as Father helped me understand this basic human relationship in a new way. I had a sense of what a father ought to be, and I could understand God's love because of this divine self-revelation to the world. God, my heavenly Father, loved me and had always loved me.

I had grown up believing that my father never loved me, yet I easily grasped the idea of an ideal father. Once I could say that I believed, I discovered inner peace when I prayed to God, my loving, caring, concerned heavenly Parent who understood me completely and guided me constantly.

Understanding the love of God enabled me to integrate other facts about that love. It also showed me the kind of love all of us need in the formative years of our lives to assist in developing a healthy self-love.

GOD'S LOVE:

- we have it unconditionally
- we can't earn it
- we don't deserve or merit it
- we can do nothing to increase it
- we can do nothing to decrease it
- we are loved for ourselves and not for what we do

Even so, many people have trouble seeing anything good about human beings. The Bible, they inform us, clearly calls us sinners. And we are sinful:

> They are corrupt, they do abominable deeds,
>   there is none that does good.

> The LORD looks down from heaven
>   upon the children of men,
>   to see if there are any that act wisely,
>   that seek after God.

> They have all gone astray, they are
>   all alike corrupt;
>   there is none that does good,
>   no, not one.
>
>   (Psalm 14:1b–3)

While the Bible speaks often of our sinfulness, it never calls us worthless. Instead, we read:

> What is man that thou art mindful of him,
> and the son of man that thou dost care for him?
>
> Yet thou hast made him little less than God,
> and dost crown him with glory and honor.
>
> (Psalm 8:4-5)

God's redemptive love shows itself to us because, instead of destroying the human creation, our Creator provided help for us in our helplessness. "But God shows his love for us in that while we were yet sinners Christ died for us" (Rom. 5:8).

We strive for righteousness (or right-standing with God), which comes only from our relationship with Jesus Christ. We don't have to do anything to become valuable. Sinful describes our defects and failures, but it does not diminish our self-worth.

For centuries pious Christians debated the value of grace as opposed to doing charitable and godly deeds, often called *works.* Our faith teaches us that God accepts us, loves us, and forever seeks to enrich us. We need to do nothing to earn or deserve God's parental love. We have value *because* God created us.

Yet most of us unconsciously still base our self-worth on the things we do and how well we perform. We find it difficult to base our worth on the fact that we are children of a God who loves us. Our Sunday schools teach us the right words, but until we experience grace in our lives we find it impossible to embrace it. We keep trying to do something—anything—that will earn God's love.

A friend named George went into the ministry, and after eight years he resigned and went into another field. I first met George at that low point in his life. He had gone through terrible internal torment because he had proved inadequate as a pastor and second-rate as a preacher.

Eventually George emerged, as another friend put it, "Like the handsome prince who had once been a frog." One day George shared with me a real insight about himself. He said, "I kept thinking that if I worked harder for God, it would make God love me more. But I never managed to do enough."

This struggle to earn our worth—and it infects many of us—goes on all the time. To love ourselves we have to understand we never do "enough."

We also face the reality that we are unable to have what we want. The dying want life and they can't have it, no matter how good they have been all their lives. No matter how positively they have thought, they still die. All their earned merit turns out to be inadequate.

Integrating

The key questions for self-worth become, Can I integrate my limitations into my sense of self-worth? Can I feel a sense of helplessness, yet still be of value? Can I believe that, as my abilities diminish, my worth as a person does not diminish?

To integrate these contrasting factors means to arrive at an understanding of our God-given value. We perceive ourselves as a mixture of capable and incapable, saint and sinner, adequate and inadequate. Integration also means we believe that the combination that is our self is valuable. We discover the true us. We already have value because God gave us that by giving us life. Integrating turns us to God for help in appreciating our value in our own eyes.

Without integration, we deceive ourselves by denying our serious defects. When we deny them, however, we also leave out part of ourselves. The part we omit is our inadequacy.

We can determine to be all that we can be, which includes the things we find unlikable. This total self-concept empowers us to discover a new kind of life previously incomprehensible.

It is a life that enables us to say without hesitation or apology, I am of value. I like being who I am.

3
Treadmill Existence

Everyone at church knows Ronald; in his town of 12,000 he is one of its best-known citizens. He serves on committees, boards, programs, and political projects. He moved into the vice-presidency of his bank at age thirty-seven.

Opinions about him differ. Some call him a conceited know-it-all because he usually does know all the facts and has the figures to back them up. Others point to his high energy level and admire his ability to do a variety of things—all of them well.

He is likable, although, so far as I am aware, no one feels close to him. He holds a master's degree in business administration and has an amazing ability to administer the most complex programs and ensure that everything goes smoothly.

I used to talk to Ronald occasionally. I sensed that he had adopted an idea common in life: that to feel important we must be doing something all the time. The more we accomplish, the more important we are.

The first time I visited his home, I walked into a den filled with plaques, emblems, scrolls, and trophies of his achievements. If I had wanted to listen, he would have told me the reason for every honor received and how hard he worked to achieve it.

I also want to tell you about Gene. We met during my college days when I joined a church in the Chicago area. Gene was probably one of the most active men in the congregation. He sang well, taught a boys' Sunday school class, and probably visited more homes than anybody else except the pastor.

The first time I talked with Gene was the Sunday he sang "The Holy City" as a solo. While not trained, his voice rang with earnestness. It touched me emotionally, and I told him so.

"Just give the glory to Jesus Christ," he said with utter sincerity. "I'm nothing but a lump of old clay. If you got blessed, God did it."

"But," I persisted, "God used your voice."

"Then give God all the praise for it," he said. "Everything I have comes from him."

For the next couple of years, I regularly heard similar phrases from Gene. When I tried to argue, he reminded me that the apostle Paul exhorted us not to think more highly of ourselves than we ought to think (e.g., Rom. 12:3). Gene interpreted that verse to mean we must think nothing of ourselves and constantly run from any admiration or praise. "I don't ever want to usurp any of God's glory," he said.

When Gene prayed, he never failed to close by saying, "And we'll be careful to give you all the praise and all the glory for all things."

Most of us label people like Gene as truly humble. They are the ones for whom we reserve the word "saint." They have a level of holiness so far beyond our own they have little appeal for us. At our most spiritual moments, we may envy them, but few of us want to imitate them.

On the other hand, we usually notice the achievers like Ronald. We sometimes admire them, envy them, reward them (with compliments at least), and wish we were like them. "How do you get so much work done?" He hears that question constantly and smiles as if he guards a secret he chooses not to share with anyone.

Sometimes we take a negative view when we look at the Ronald types. "Is he stuck on himself!" "No conceit in his family; he has it all." "He goes around acting as if he owns the whole world."

Despite the sarcastic words, Ronald provides the role model for most of us. He gets the job done! He achieves! He may be smug and even self-centered, but wouldn't we all like to be like him? At least a little? We rise to his defense by quoting, "It ain't bragging if you can do it."

To complete my story about these two men, I saw a different

side at a later time when they each faced serious problems. Long after my college days, I moved away, and then Gene's oldest son died in a plane crash. A few days after the boy's funeral, the two of us talked quietly in his backyard at sunset.

As Gene watched the descending darkness, he said, "That's how I feel sometimes. Like all the light is going out of my life." A few minutes later he said, "You know, I try so hard to be what God wants me to be, but I always fail. Will I ever get to the place in my life where I can live a life that honors him?" Gene believed he never measured up to whatever he assumed God expected of him. He felt self-contempt because he could never live up to his own ideals.

I visited Ronald in the hospital after a near-fatal heart attack at age forty-nine. While I don't recall his exact words, they sounded strangely like those of Gene. Ronald saw his life nearing an end and realized how little he had done and how unfaithful he had been to God. I was tempted to point out to him that he probably did more for God than most church members, but he probably wouldn't have understood. Ronald set his own standards, and by them he had failed.

Life on a Treadmill

Recently, I thought of these two men and realized how much alike they were in one respect. Both lived a treadmill existence. They kept running, rushing, throwing all their energies into their activities. Yet neither had a healthy self-appreciation. Neither man really loved himself. Whether we label one a man of self-contempt and the other a conceited person, they both point to a similar inadequacy. Neither valued himself or loved himself for who he was.

That should be no great surprise. Following the philosophy of our culture means that our life operates on a treadmill. We never get anywhere. We know only that we must keep at it. We find importance by expending our energies. We gain significance by what we produce. We have to show that we are working hard. Others respect economic success, prestige, power, and acquisition as symbols of our significance.

This standard tends to make the ordinary less meaningful.

Those who don't achieve the upper rungs have less value. The individuals who quit climbing the ladder, we treat with disdain. When the woman says, "I'm *only* a housewife," she views herself as being of lesser worth than her husband, who brings home "real money."

To be important, we must feel important. We feel important when we're working hard or doing something worthwhile. Those who have feelings of inadequacy discover that they can often cover up by working harder. Their increased efforts often gain the respect of the world around them.

"That woman sure has it together."

"He's really going places!"

"He has it made."

And yet . . .

One way to see the futility of increased effort is to consider the couple who work hard all their lives, trying to get ahead so they can enjoy their retirement years. Yet within two years after retirement one of them becomes seriously ill, dies, and the other is left alone. In anguish the grieving survivor says, "It isn't fair!"

Such individuals have lost their sense of value as people. They are no longer productive. They finally ask, What am I? What am I worth? Isn't there something more than this treadmill existence?

That term itself, treadmill existence, explains the attitude of many people in our society. We keep trying for more. We strive to achieve. But, like running on a treadmill, we ultimately discover that we don't get anywhere.

One seventy-year-old woman who had worked since she was thirteen told me, "I'm not good for anything except to be thrown on the garbage heap."

By contrast, the biblical concept looks at life differently. A good way to state it is: *We are, therefore we are important.*

When God chose the Israelites for a special people, Moses told them it had nothing to do with their size or their importance; "it is because the LORD loves you, and is keeping the oath which he swore to your fathers, that the LORD has brought you out with a mighty hand, and redeemed you from the house of bondage" (Deut. 7:8). Their value to God came about because of their existence.

Five Principles

In reflecting on Ronald and Gene I have come to five conclusions about self-love, or self-esteem, which can be stated in the form of principles.

1. Because we are God's creation, we are important. We find this assertion difficult to understand and even more difficult to accept. Our culture does not reward us for simply *being,* but smiles upon us for our achievements.

For instance, in the early 1980s, the farm-equipment industry had all but shut down. When the companies laid off men who were heads of households, they survived during the period of unemployment benefits. But when the money stopped, they crumbled emotionally.

One morning I heard four couples interviewed on television. Each husband admitted he felt "less than a man" because he couldn't support his family. They spoke of depression and confusion. One man admitted he had been drinking heavily. In two cases, the wives were supporting the families while their husbands waited for jobs to turn up. These same men who had a sense of value when they brought in weekly paychecks no longer had any value in their own eyes.

2. We are unable to accept God's love for us as we are. One tragedy of original sin is that we cannot accept who we are, and so we struggle compulsively to change ourselves into who we want to be. If we want respect, we think we must earn it. If we want love, we must prove our worthiness to be loved. If we want acceptance, we must show others that we are acceptable.

Sally Field received her second Oscar for her role in the film *Places in the Heart.* In her acceptance speech, she gushed, "You love me! You really love me!" Her words seemed to say that she based her self-worth on the validation of receiving the highest honor in her profession. But what will happen when she does not win? Does that mean she's unloved? Worthless?

Because of our inability to accept ourselves as important, we follow the pattern of our original parents. Like them, we hide. And even when we are well hidden, we still wonder why we feel isolated, alienated, separated. Worse, we find it difficult to believe that God can and does extend love to us, even in our worst moments of disobedience.

This story of the garden took on a richness one day for Vern when his two-year-old son, Brian, was playing in the next room. Brian dropped a heavy toy on top of a glass-topped coffee table, and there was a loud crash.

Vern called, "Brian!" as he raced toward the room to find out what had happened. Brian, however, knew he had broken the glass, heard his father's voice, and raced out of the room, down the hallway, and into his own room.

Vern watched his son disappear, thinking of how the child's fear and disobedience broke the relationship between them (Brian knew he should not be playing with toys near the table). The boy, hiding in his room, felt isolated and alone.

As a father Vern knew he could be angry and still love his son. He also felt sad, realizing that Brian didn't know that he had broken the relationship.

"It reminded me of Eden," Vern said. "I pictured God walking in the garden. God's children heard their names called but they didn't answer. They broke the relationship and felt the terrible sense of estrangement. God never changed toward them."

As parents we know we still love our children when they disobey. But children sometimes fear that their disobedience will lead to punishment and, even worse, the withdrawing of love because they perceive they no longer deserve it.

When we have an inadequate view of ourselves—either thinking too much or too little—it distorts our self-perception. It results in a sense of aloneness and a lack of intimacy. To avoid our estrangement, we feverishly play a variety of roles. We define ourselves as husband or wife, parent or child, by our occupation or church affiliation. Too often, these roles take on the meaning that belongs to our being itself. We revert from one to another, but never step away from them to know who we are behind the roles.

We're needy inside, and we do all kinds of things to have those needs filled. Ronald tried one method and Gene another. Both were defective, yet they kept trying to *do* something to achieve what was already theirs.

3. *We find it hard to become vulnerable, and when we do, we*

label it bad. We assume that since we feel alone, guilty, un-fulfilled, or empty we are bad—or at least ineffectual. If we were all right we are sure we would not need anything.

Both Gene and Ronald became vulnerable at one point in their lives. Instead of allowing the event to become a positive moment for change, they tagged their feelings as negative, bad, and un-wanted.

Again, in the Garden of Eden story, the couple disobeyed God. Suddenly they had knowledge and looked at themselves and saw they were naked. They had been naked all along, but now they became aware of it and could no longer tolerate themselves as they were. They had not changed—except they knew how to disobey and they understood the emotions of shame and guilt. Their first act was to clothe themselves in fig leaves. They could not remain as they were.

They made decisions about what was good and what was bad. They decided that nakedness was bad. They hid from God be-cause they saw themselves as bad. They became aware of their vulnerability—not realizing they had been just as vulnerable be-fore their disobedience. Now their vulnerability took on the connotation of wrongness.

When we human beings take it upon ourselves to decide what is good and what is not, we usurp God's role. All of us experience loneliness, limitations, and emptiness. Unfortunately, we strike out against them. Our temptation, as in the garden, is to say that we know what is good and what is bad. We equate the painful with bad and the pleasurable with good.

We find it difficult to be aware of our isolation from others and then to label that as good or part of being human. So we spend a lot of energy trying to avoid isolation from others. Janice exem-plified this idea when she sought counseling over her failing marriage. She had grown up with the idea that marriage would be *the* fulfilling event in her life. "I never realized that marriage could be lonely even though we love each other." She had ex-pected her husband to make her a complete person, without any needs, because of the relationship—a demand no human could ever fulfill. She labeled her marriage "bad" because of his limita-tion.

Janice continues in her struggle to understand that marriage cannot totally fulfill her. Feelings of loneliness and isolation are part of the human condition. Her therapist told her, "You first have to be complete in yourself before you can be happily married. Being complete says you accept that you are limited and incomplete."

4. *When we seek approval validated by external means, we end up doing something to prove, earn, evoke, or force it.* Some seek acceptance in reverse by being labeled the "-est"—the meanest, the biggest, the greatest, even the roughest. These superlatives offer us uniqueness even if it's a negative uniqueness.

Such individuals manipulate situations to bring about actions by others that result in giving them validation.

However, if we want true validation we begin with accepting ourselves. We have to strip away the fig leaves and let people look at our inner nakedness. Otherwise they love our good qualities but don't know the real us. If they don't know the real us, how can they love us?

To consider how this works, think about pastors. During my years in that role, I believed that most parishioners expected me to be on call at all hours, forever eager to help, never giving up when discovering needy individuals. Several times I discussed this with other clergy, who felt the same way.

At some of our low moments we asked one another, Are we loved for ourselves? Or for what we do for others? Would we still be held in respect, even veneration, if we did only what our job descriptions specifically stated? Many of us wondered, Does this extra effort reflect true valuing of myself or—as we probed deeper—does it reflect my trying to prove my value to myself and to others?

When I finally asked myself this last question I didn't like the answer. It did, however, start me on the road to discover that my true value as a person came as a gift from God. It took time for me to appreciate that I am of value simply because I exist. Slowly I realized that, out of my value as a human being, along with the gifts God gave me, I could help people in need. During the last two years of my pastorate, my ministry did not particularly change. I changed. I still did essentially what I had always done. Yet I worked from a sense of self-worth and not to earn self-worth.

5. *Outward behavior alone does not show how we feel about ourselves.* Long working hours, high productivity, or accumulation of wealth tell us nothing directly. The behavior that emerges when we feel loved can look similar to the behavior of those who are trying to earn love.

Any time we purposefully give a good impression (as contrasted with a true picture), we are avoiding honesty. We are trying to be someone we are not. We can't love ourselves until we learn to become relentlessly truthful about ourselves.

Pastors who respond to the needs of others can be just as vulnerable in needing to prove themselves as anybody else. From the outside we can't tell where those qualities we admire—such as self-giving, self-sacrifice, compassion, and concern—originate.

If we truly like ourselves, we may behave like Ronald and other strivers, but with a different basis for our action. We don't have to prove our importance; we function *out of* our importance. We don't live on a treadmill. Instead we produce, because we know our Creator-Lover-God has endowed us with abilities to accomplish certain tasks.

Once we know our value to God, we step off the treadmill. We can become productive. We have abilities. We have opportunities to help others. We please God by using these talents.

In discussing self-love in a support group, one member described his life by saying that each role he played was like the skin of an onion. "If you strip them all away one at a time, eventually there's nothing left and I am a nothing."

I answered, "I'd rather use the image of the artichoke. You keep pulling away the leaves and finally you reach the artichoke heart. That's the best part."

I really believe that. As long as we have life in us we are still of value, no matter how reduced our roles or our abilities.

4

Valuing Helplessness

Three experiences helped Vern to change his understanding about self-love radically. All three stories deal with loss. Although we have changed their names, each of the people in these experiences took him a little farther in his appreciation for the value of helplessness.

He learned that losses and pain are hard enough to deal with by themselves. Most of us also feel that we are less valuable in such circumstances because we produce less.

Annie and Eunice

Vern met Annie and Eunice on his rounds as a chaplain in a hospice. One woman had stayed alert but the other had lost her vitality. In talking to them he learned the similarities of their histories. Both were incontinent. Both had developed cataracts. Both were bound to wheelchairs. Both were the last surviving member of their families and their circles of friends. Yet Annie remained vibrant and fun to visit, while Eunice had already died inside. They approached their lives, their aging, and their dying in fundamentally different ways.

He asked Annie, "How can you enjoy life so much in your condition?"

"It's in God's hands," Annie said. "I left it there a long time ago." Then she told him her story. When she was a young girl she had enjoyed running more than anything else. (She was forty years ahead of her time.) But, in her twenties, a traffic accident left her permanently in a wheelchair. She felt the unfairness of life. Her anger flared up at everything because life had marred her. "Finally," Annie said, "after all that, I decided to see what was left of my life."

Although Annie could not explain how this happened, she learned to focus on living as well as she could instead of staying focused on what she did not have. She maintained that philosophy to the end of her life.

When faced with other tragic events, any one of which could have totally crushed her, Annie reacted to the pain and the loss realistically. After she grieved over her new loss, she would then ask herself, "How can I live the rest of my life?" This simple affirmation of life kept her vitally connected.

By contrast, Eunice faced equally painful losses. Each time she repeated the same statements: "I've been a good woman and tried to live right all my life. Why should this happen to me when all those other people have no troubles?"

Her time in a wheelchair started much later than Annie's, but she had lost her husband and all the members of her family. Her eyesight and hearing were fading. She didn't have anybody to visit her. As each of these losses took place, she kept saying, "This isn't fair. This isn't right." She became increasingly bitter and angry.

Externally both women suffered pain and loss. The difference lay not in their circumstances but in their perceptions of their lives. One woman was stuck in the past. The other lived in the present.

Eunice concentrated on life's unfairness in anger, grief, and self-pity. Those are all natural feelings, but she never learned to get beyond them.

Barbara and Tom

The second story concerns Tom and Barbara's marriage of twenty years. They have one teenage child and one child in elementary school. Their marriage started out romantic and happy. Tom earned a good income and became increasingly successful. Barbara enjoyed caring for the children and the house.

Then, almost imperceptibly, the satisfaction each got out of that arrangement faded.

Barbara realized she did not want to be the person Tom wanted her to remain. While she enjoyed being a parent she didn't want to be *only* a parent. She began to feel trapped and wanted to get outside the confines of their home.

When they first married it was terribly important to her to have security. She wanted to own a house they could be proud of and to have a good standard of living. She kept their home spotless, and their yard, blooming with flowers and shrubs throughout the year, was the envy of the neighborhood.

Tom also changed. By middle age he disliked going out to social affairs. He wanted to spend more time in his basement workshop or watching sports telecasts.

While Tom needed less, Barbara needed more. No longer content as only a parent and housewife, she involved herself in the community. She took on heavier responsibilities at her church. Over a two-year period, Barbara changed drastically.

The more she changed, the more uneasy it made Tom. He felt her new attitudes threatened the stability of their marriage. On the outside people did not see any difference. Tom and Barbara remained one of the community's model couples.

On the inside, though, Tom became angry. "I don't even know you anymore," he said. "You're not the Barbara I married. I want the old Barbara back!"

As his anger increased, he started demanding more. Tom interpreted each change Barbara made as her way of abandoning him, the children, and their life-style. He reacted by alternating between sullenness and belligerence. He wanted everything to stay the way it had been. "We had such a good life," he reminded her.

As Tom's rage increased, Barbara withdrew from him. He received less attention and affection. When Barbara became sexually unavailable, that infuriated him. He tried everything he knew to get his wife to be the woman he wanted her to be.

They have been in therapy for over a year. Neither wants to end the marriage, yet neither is willing to give in to the other's demands. Neither can accept anything less than total capitulation from the other.

It's easy to call Tom the bad guy, but it's more complicated than that. All of us get caught in the midst of change. Like Tom and Barbara, we often don't know what to do or how to relate to those with whom we were once so intimate.

Tom feels a sense of loss and wants life to be the way it used to be. Barbara feels loss too. But for her to remain as she was would be a greater loss. Both want life their way; neither can accept the other's choice.

Thelma

Thelma is a middle-aged parent. She lost two children at birth. After that, because she believed something was wrong with her body, she saw herself as a little less than a "real" woman.

Eventually she and her husband adopted two children. The first child, Terry, was extremely bright and capable, and she really enjoyed raising him. He started to read at age three. At school he always stood out academically and socially. But when Terry turned fifteen, he quietly rebelled. His grades dropped. He turned moody. He lied to Thelma about where he spent his spare time.

Aside from the fact that Terry had entered that adolescent stage of life when he didn't even understand himself, something more significant took place. Terry, bright and independent, did not need or want Thelma's mother-smother.

She, however, could not adjust to this abrupt change. She was sure she knew who this child ought to be and how he ought to behave. Her previous losses made her fearful and overly protective. She lectured him daily. She told him how he was disappointing her, his father, and even the grandparents.

"I don't know what I did wrong," Thelma would wail. "I tried to raise you up right." No matter how much he tried to reassure his mother that she had not failed to do anything for him, Thelma could not believe him. Terry's reversal to his former compliant self would be the only acceptable proof.

Thelma linked her identity integrally with how she saw her child perform. She weighed the boy down with the burden of her own self-esteem.

The loss she faced when Terry turned out to be different from the son she wanted reflected on her own sense of being a competent mother.

In the middle of the ongoing crisis with Terry, Thelma was confronting a situation with her daughter.

Angela, the second adopted child, turned out to have significant learning difficulties. This problem threatened Thelma even more. It became a major trial for her to raise this nearly uncontrollable child who was suffering inside. To her credit she reached Angela. But to do that she had to accept the truth that her child's behavior did not reflect on herself, either as a person or as a mother. She finally learned that she could not allow Angela's disabilities to determine her own self-worth.

Avoiding Helplessness

All these people suffered loss, and all of them felt helpless: Annie and Eunice, Barbara and Tom, Thelma. But Annie, Barbara, and Thelma have learned to value life, even when it does not shower joy and apparent success at every corner.

All of us feel empty spots as we experience our fundamental separateness from other people. Even at the height of success, something is still lacking. Praise, applause, appreciation, affirmation—whatever we get from others—is never enough. We always want more.

Because we don't get enough, we feel our estrangement from others. This separateness initially feels bad, the loss of no longer being joined, the facing of our aloneness.

Feeling our separateness scares us. We do all kinds of things to avoid facing it. Some marry to fill the emptiness; others join groups. Some throw themselves feverishly into their work. Some become sexually promiscuous. Others try "recreational" drugs.

Some of us begin to feel our incompleteness and blame our parents, saying that they never gave enough love, attention, understanding—however we express it. We want to convince ourselves that somehow there's a way to feel whole.

We eventually learn that blaming parents doesn't serve a useful purpose in escaping our helplessness. Neither do drugs, heavy workloads, or changing sexual partners. Marriage disillusions us because we don't get filled up there, either. We learn that, except for brief moments of intimacy, our partners can't fill the emptiness that is in our lives.

Until we accept our own loneliness, emptiness, limitations, and incompleteness, we put enormous pressure on the people we believe ought to fulfill us. Consciously or unconsciously, we demand that they become the people we need rather than accept them as they are. They, too, are also empty and needy.

Accepting Helplessness

Annie, Barbara, and Thelma all grew. They learned to accept the vicissitudes that life handed them, following the adage "If life hands you a lemon, make lemonade." However, many people do not know how to do that. But some do. They inspire us, and they also point out to us that we can accept our losses. We can even value our helplessness.

Vern learned this life truth initially by working with hospice patients like Annie. He talked with these patients, visited their rooms, and watched how they responded to life.

They had to depend on others for everything. They could not walk, urinate, eat, or do a hundred other things without help. Yet most of them did not cry out in despair or lie in silent depression. They understood their situation and, although they would not have said it this way, they grasped the value of helplessness.

They didn't choose to depend on others. They would have preferred to be living independently. Yet once aware of their deteriorating physical condition and impending death, they accepted their situation. Most of them made the best of what life still offered. Even more, they manifested a positive outlook.

Observing and working with these patients each day helped Vern to understand the world around him. He came to see helplessness as an integral part of our human condition.

Even in the hospice, he recognized those who capitalized on their situation. Some people used their helplessness expertly to manipulate others.

We need not throw up our hands and abdicate responsibility for our lives. Helplessness means that we find ourselves in positions where we can do nothing for ourselves. It is as if we were infants again, depending on the love and care of others.

It's where we might ask, When I can't do anything for myself, am I still somebody? When I have no practical value left, am I worthwhile? If I can't do anything for anyone else, or even myself, am I still worth loving?

We question who we are when we lose the roles and activities that previously defined us. While those activities have been important, they're not sufficient to provide us with self-worth. This especially applies in the process of aging. We end up helpless, dependent, with virtually no means of affecting our world and no control over our lives.

Are we then of value? In the secular view the answer to that question is no or, at best, a qualified yes. (In some primitive societies, they killed the elderly who no longer functioned in expected roles.) From the religious view, we shout, "Yes! You are still valuable!"

Suppose I trained to be a surgeon. I might be the most skilled surgeon in the world, yet I would still confront instances where I couldn't do anything. Some bodies defy repair. All of us, no matter what our position in life, encounter such moments. No matter how hard we try, we cannot make everything happen the way we want it. If we face ourselves honestly, we have to recognize and admit our helplessness.

Our society tempts us to confess that we can do anything if we throw ourselves fully into it. We said we were going to land on the moon and we did. We found cures for polio and hundreds of other diseases. Our communications world blazes since the invention of the microchip. These breakthroughs make us confident that if we apply all of our technical expertise to a problem, we can eventually solve it.

As long as we maintain that kind of thinking, we will never understand helplessness. We despise our weaknesses, hide our inconsistencies, and bewail our inability to do more or to be more perfect. With those attitudes, we can't love ourselves.

Instead of loving ourselves and admitting that we are both good and bad, skilled and unskilled, we boast of our abilities and deny or despise ourselves because of what we lack.

In the Bible we see this clearly in Paul's self-revelation in Romans 7. All through that monumental letter he discussed the Mosaic law and showed its inadequacy to save. The law made people aware of what they couldn't do. It showed them their sinfulness and convicted them of wrongdoing, but it never offered salvation.

> I do not understand my own actions. For I do not do what I want, but I do the very thing I hate. Now if I do what I do not want, I agree that the law is good. So then it is no longer I that do it, but sin which dwells within me. For I know that nothing good dwells within me, that is, in my flesh. I can will what is right, but I cannot do it. For if I do not do the good I want, but the evil I do not want is what I do. Now if I do what I do not want, it is no longer I that do it, but sin which dwells with me.
>
> So I find it to be a law that when I want to do right, evil lies close at hand. For I delight in the law of God, in my inmost self, but I see in my members another law at war with the law of my mind and making me captive to the law of sin which dwells in my members. Wretched man that I am! Who will deliver me from this body of death? Thanks be to God through Jesus Christ our Lord! So then, I of myself serve the law of God with my mind, but with my flesh I serve the law of sin.
>
> There is therefore now no condemnation for those who are in Christ Jesus.
>
> (Romans 7:15–8:1)

Paul's words depict despair, confusion, helplessness—all signs of his inability to be and to do everything he knows of as good. It is only when he cries out in despair, "Who will deliver me?" that he comes to the right answer. He turns to Jesus Christ. Once we are "in" Jesus Christ, we are free from the condemnation, confusion, and helplessness that Paul depicts.

Starting with helplessness enables us to reexamine life from a different perspective. We face our inability to do everything we need or want to do. As long as we excuse ourselves or cover up our helplessness, we run from the truth.

Valuing Helplessness

When we move beyond merely accepting our helplessness, we come into a place where we value our helplessness. That puts us in a position to learn to love ourselves.

We have trouble praying, *God, help me understand that helpless-*

*ness, loneliness, emptiness, and limitations are part of your loving crea-
tion.* Yet they are.

Those who live long enough usually come to the conclusion
that they have value in just being alive. This leads us to say that
all of us are divine creations and God requires only that we be
ourselves.

Judith Viorst gets at the heart of this idea when she writes, in
Necessary Losses:

> Losing is the price we pay for living. It is also the source of much
> of our growth and gain. Making our way from birth to death, we
> also have to make our way through the pain of giving up and giving
> up and giving up some portion of what we cherish.
>
> We have to deal with our necessary losses.
>
> We should understand how these losses are linked to our gains.
>
> For in leaving the blurred-boundary bliss of mother-child one-
> ness, we become a conscious, unique and separate self, exchanging
> the illusion of absolute shelter and absolute safety for the trium-
> phant anxieties of standing alone.
>
> And in bowing to the forbidden and the impossible, we become
> a moral, responsible, adult self, discovering—within the limitations
> imposed by necessity—our freedoms and choices.
>
> And in giving up our impossible expectations, we become a
> lovingly connected self, renouncing ideal visions of perfect friend-
> ship, marriage, children, family life for the sweet imperfections of
> all-too-human relationships.

Understanding the reality about ourselves and others frees us
to love the imperfect and the needy. And we begin this by loving
ourselves.

We have the great example of God's love for us:

> While we were still weak, at the right time Christ died for the
> ungodly. Why, one will hardly die for a righteous man—though
> perhaps for a good man one will dare even to die. But God shows
> his love for us in that while we were yet sinners Christ died for us.
> (Romans 5:6–8)

We cannot love until we face our own sinfulness. Otherwise we
remain like demanding children who become outraged when
their needs are not met. We blame others for failing to give **us**
fulfillment.

We normally translate worth and value into feeling good. If we feel good about ourselves, we consider ourselves to be of value. Unfortunately, we can't hold on to feeling good. Our emotions come and go.

If, however, we learn to value all our feelings as part of our true selves, we have taken a major step toward learning to love ourselves. It may seem contradictory to include failure, disappointment, helplessness, and loneliness as part of goodness. Yet these qualities are part of us—the parts difficult to live with.

Furthermore, to be loved we must be willing to be helpless. We must allow others to bestow love. At the same time, we cannot make somebody send us a birthday card, much less love us. We can try any number of manipulations—ranging from inducing guilt or pity to intimidation—to try to coerce others to respond to us the way we want. All these attempts deny our limitations and others' free choice. Love is nurturing only when it is given freely.

Although some actions pass for love, anything not given freely results from our manipulation. We earn it or manage to bring it about.

When we realize our helplessness to make people love us, we can then receive the gift instead of wondering if we could manipulate them into giving it to us. That's when helplessness becomes a key to loving and to our own self-esteem.

To value helplessness as part of life and as part of being God's loving creation is never easy. Yet as we go on our journey toward loving ourselves, we never quite make it without accepting these truths.

5

The Divine Option

"It's in God's hands," wrinkled old Annie said. "I left it there a long time ago." Nothing in the way she said the words or the expression on her face caused Vern to doubt her sincerity.

Annie was only one of several who spoke that way. By then he had been working for four months with hospice patients. He kept hearing similar statements again and again.

These people knew they were dying. The first few times Vern heard them say such words, he felt skeptical. He wondered if they repeated their religious phrases as a way to avoid pain or from an unwillingness to accept their losses. Nobody could be that calm, he reasoned, especially in the face of the loss and pain these people had to face.

Some of these expressions of faith of course were a way to avoid pain, but many reflected a wisdom and faith that Vern had yet to experience.

In time Vern learned they were wiser than he. They had discovered—with real understanding—that some things in life are beyond our control. No matter how hard we try or how much we produce, we cannot change them. Vern had always known intellectually what they demonstrated in their living.

He learned other things, too. They didn't live in anticipation of the next day but accepted each day as it came. They helped him to understand that no matter what we do or how hard we work we cannot change God's love for us. The confidence that such a God exists allows people with that caliber of faith to focus on what they can manage. They can let go of the things they cannot handle. Faith allows them to face their mortality, to live while they can, and to cope daily with the pain of losing their life.

Although Vern learned this valuable lesson of faith from hospice patients, he observed it just as clearly in Alcoholics Anonymous (AA) and other groups such as Al-Anon, Overeaters Anonymous, and Gamblers Anonymous, which use the same twelve-step approach. The programs stress spirituality and accepting each day as it comes. They stress catchy terms such as "Let go and let God" or "Easy does it."

On one occasion Vern visited an AA group and heard Marcia tell her story. "I am forty-two years old," she said. "Two days ago I got back the lab reports. I have metastasized breast cancer."

She understood exactly what the diagnosis meant as well as the prognosis. She added, "I feel like denying this, that it's not happening to me but to somebody else. But it *is* happening to me. I've been praying for God to help me face whatever lies ahead."

Her last statement became the key to understanding the rest. Marcia and thousands of others acknowledge a Higher Power, what we call God. Their acknowledgment says that God is greater than we are and knows more than we do.

Few of us will escape a confrontation with pain and suffering. Most of us will not know why. We can't always make sense out of the world. Yet we can live each day still believing God cares for us and is with us.

The Divine Option

During this same period, Vern sat in a worship service where they sang "He Leadeth Me." Vern had long ago put aside songs like this because of their sentimentality and simplistic theology.

That day he listened—really listened—as the people around him sang all four stanzas. That song presents God as leading us every day and in every circumstance. The final stanza speaks of death and life beyond.

He realized that faith means that we can face our greatest fears. We can lose everything, including our lives, yet still trust that God leads us, that even at death and beyond we are safe.

To come to such an understanding requires a confrontation

with our human limitations, our less-than-Godness. We have to acknowledge that, ultimately, we are not in control of our fate. When our lives depend on things such as our productivity and on what we do, we falsely assume that we can control how we will live.

When faced with helplessness, powerlessness, loneliness, and other human limitations, we are forced to admit our lack of control. That self-honesty gives us the power to live and to feel positively about ourselves. Until we can acknowledge our frailty, we confront predicaments alone and fight losing battles.

To have confidence that we are important and worthwhile when we're in positions where we have no control and must depend on others for everything is a kind of faith many have not yet learned to understand. That's what we call the Divine Option.

The Divine Option means acknowledging two things: we live in a world we don't fully understand, and we live in a world created by a loving God.

Stripped of Worth

When we insist on being the master of our lives, our self-esteem depends on our success. If nothing exists bigger than we are, and if circumstances rip our accomplishments from us, we feel that we have failed. Failure diminishes us in our own eyes. That usually leads to sadness, anger, and depression. We see ourselves stripped of all worth and therefore valueless.

Our worth too often becomes contingent upon activities, productivity, roles that we play or that are vital to our functioning. We wouldn't deny the importance of those activities and our productivity. Yet eventually we lose the externals. We need a firm foundation so that our self-esteem remains intact when life strips everything else away.

Some people never face losses in their lives. They rush ahead too fast and ignore the realities around them. If we live long enough, we start losing. Our friends die. We retire or lose our jobs. Aging takes many things away. Divorce happens. Our children grow up and leave. We finally begin to realize the many factors we cannot control.

If we make a conscious commitment to deal with life's losses as they come, our ability to cope is strengthened. And we can learn to do so.

For instance, most of us could change a tire, even if we had never seen a car before. Given enough time, we would figure it out. But with a set of directions, even though we'd never changed a tire before, we could change the tire a lot faster. And if we've changed tires on other vehicles, we know how it's done. We might bang a knuckle or two, but we could change the tire without too much difficulty.

The same is true with facing limits, losses, immortality, even living. All of us will have to deal with these realities. For most of us, if we have enough time we will cope constructively with the losses in our lives. If, however, we have a set of directions, a way of thinking, or especially if we have faith, we will probably fare better. If we add experience and practice in dealing with our limitations, we have the best chance of coping with our pain. We have faith that we will eventually figure it out—just like changing a tire.

When tragedies strike—a child dies, our mate leaves—we feel the blow. We still have something to rely on. We have lost something valuable but we have not lost our self-value. Losses are painful, but they are not statements about our worth.

We must remember that self-worth belongs to us by simply being ourselves. We are valuable to God because we are alive.

We may not seem to be of much use. (And when we talk about being of use we are again missing the point.) We exist. God declares that to be alive is to have value.

Why?

When things happen that we don't understand, we tend to spend our energies in trying to figure them out.

"This isn't fair!" "It's not right." "How come it's this way?"

Although these are valid questions, they often lead us nowhere. Vern has worked with clients who kept asking, "Why was it that way?" Even if they could explain *why* in graphic detail, that understanding still wouldn't help them cope with *what is.* Knowing the reason does not alter the event.

If we compare what happens in our lives with what we understand about God, we may complain, "God must be a real manipulator who's just jerking me around." If we go further, we can say, "This is a God who loves me even though I don't understand why these things happen. Despite my lack of understanding I'm determined to live today." That way we're freer, and we truly live each day instead of spending our energy figuring out why things happen as they do.

Questions about why things happen may have value. Sometimes learning some of the whys helps people to let go of the issue so that they can get on with living.

Once we become aware of our value, we're ready to discover how we can use what's left of our lives. We have a divine obligation to be all that we can be. God expects us to develop our talents and our creativity and to make use of our opportunities.

Nowhere in the New Testament does this appear more poignantly than in the parable Jesus told about the master who went on a journey and entrusted three servants with varying amounts of money (Matt. 25:14–30). The first two multiplied their capital. The third, a fearful man, buried his and kept it safe. When the master returned, the third had no increase to show, and the master berated him.

This parable helps us see our responsibility to be as fully who we are as possible. We're obligated to use what we have. To bury our abilities through disuse is to fail God and ourselves. Using our abilities involves taking risks, trusting that somehow God protects us and is concerned about us even when we're in the midst of the impossible.

Making Sense

Life doesn't always make sense. A hundred things occur for which we never have explanations. Part of our commitment to the Divine Option says that no matter how little we understand of what happens, we still trust.

Let's say we're resentful about not getting enough affection from our mother. Eventually we learn that Mom was not happy, and she had a lot of family stress to contend with. Mom learned how to be dutiful but not demonstrative. She may have performed inadequately. Understanding Mom helps us realize that our lack of receiving affection doesn't point to a defect in our character. We see it is as part of the reality of our lives.

We can either accept what we learn and say, "That's the way it was; I can't change it," and focus our energies on the question, "How am I going to live today?" Or, even knowing Mom better, we can harbor resentment and blame her for not giving us what we wanted.

We have to decide. We learn to live and love better when we believe that God lovingly created our world and we don't have to understand everything that happens.

It's hard to believe in God's love when we feel banged around by the world. If we based our evaluation of God's being loving only on our own experiences, we might have difficulty in coming to a positive conclusion. If, however, we consider the experience of others, the testimony of the Bible, and view our lives a little less subjectively, God emerges as loving. We can take this broader look despite the painful and unanswered questions that remain. Even unanswered questions don't have to keep us from living today.

For example, Vern's twenty-year-old brother died of cancer when Vern was twenty-four. Vern found his death incomprehensible. Yet in his grief Vern affirmed, in a greater way than ever, his belief in a God who is loving even though twenty-year-olds die.

As one consequence of his brother's death, Vern decided to prepare for the ministry. Until that point, his grappling with faith revolved around making sense out of life. He didn't find immediate answers and he's still not sure about a lot of things. But he did discover that living and loving are worthwhile even if life includes loss, separation, death, and tragedy.

Vern didn't arrive at a logical conclusion. Without sufficient evidence, and in a time of feeling the pain and unfairness of life, he discovered faith in a loving God. The biblical passages used at the funeral, words he previously dismissed as irrelevant, sustained him in his moments of chaos and pain. At the same time, others around Vern faced the same loss and said, "It's not fair."

His brother's death wasn't fair by any understanding Vern had. Yet the ability to believe that life was worthwhile (and ultimately that Vern, too, had value) even in the face of that kind of pain was, for him, an illogical yet real leap of faith. Only years later could he begin to talk about it.

I have a friend who sometimes says, "It's not logical but it makes sense." That's one way to describe Vern's experience. We all encounter inexplicable events that we can't understand. If we demand to understand them, we can't get on with the business of living. If we persist in yelling, "It's not fair!" we stay enmeshed in that struggle.

Many things aren't fair, and others don't make sense. We can't even prove that anything ultimately makes sense. If we reach beyond the chaos, this understanding comes to us as a sudden insight or an amazing discovery. We can never explain *how* something happens, only that it does happen.

If we can internalize the reality that we are loved even though we're inadequate, in pain, and making serious errors, we don't have to find logical proof. We don't have to find rational explanations as to how we can be loved when we're so flawed.

Anybody who's been a parent knows that it's possible to love that messy, screaming, imperfect creature called *my child*. It isn't necessary to explain how we can love someone who kept us up most of the night changing diapers or trying to get a fever down. We can think of God's loving us in a similar way. That's the Divine Option. That's the conscious connection with a God who loves us.

When people say they have trouble committing themselves to a God who allows innocent children to die of starvation, who permits wars to wipe out millions, who refuses to destroy the wicked, I can never offer a rational explanation. Maybe my words don't convince them either. Yet deep within me, it makes sense. But then, I have turned to the Divine Option.

Exercise

Vern uses a device to help clients learn of their own self-worth and to see this as coming from God. Try this simple exercise.

1. Make a list of the qualities you would insist upon from a God who would want to listen to you. Answering questions like these will help you in making the list:

Do I want my God to be male or female? Does it matter?
What will my God look like?
Will my God be stern with me when I fail? Gentle?
Will my God listen to me?
How will my God remind me that I'm not making sense? That I'm being self-deceptive? That I'm failing?

2. For at least two minutes a day—and for some people that can seem a long time—pray to that God. Here's a way to pray, if you want a God who listens.

God, thanks for listening to me. You're always open to me, and that means a lot. I have friends but I can't always depend on them. But you're always there.

3. Once you have established the habit of daily prayer, move on to the following three steps:

(a) Present yourself to God as fully and as honestly as you can. You might say things such as *I'm in a good mood* or *I'm distrustful.*

(b) Acknowledge things in your life for which you are truly thankful, such as *I'm grateful for———* or *I'm thankful you———.*

(c) Ask for a knowledge of God's will, such as *Show me how to———.*

This exercise can be helpful because many of us grew up with the idea of a remote God who makes pronouncements about who we are. Those pronouncements may include:

"You're lovable."

"I sent Jesus to die for you because of my love for you."

"I made a good world. You're part of the world and that makes you good."

Yet such statements often are not enough. We need to touch, hear, and see our God. We need a flesh-and-blood contact. That's why we celebrate the incarnation—Jesus became a true human to help us understand the true nature of God.

Some of us grew up with the ingrained (and often hidden) concept of God as the great scorekeeper in the sky. Others view God as the one who created the world, set it in motion, and then retired from the scene while we messed it up. With such views, it's easy to feel, as one person said, "My prayers reach no further than the top of my head."

No matter how we envision God, this exercise will enable us

to enter into a relationship with a caring God who is concerned about our welfare.

If we've gone through the exercise faithfully when we hit times of chaos, we can talk to God. We can say, *Listen, God, you don't seem close to me lately. Things have gone rotten and I don't like it. You said we could ask and receive guidance. I need your help to make sense of what's going on around me. Help me to want to follow your will.*

Many people have found this exercise helpful. When we pray, the act itself acknowledges that we are not in charge. Prayer confesses that we need help and we are placing our lives at God's disposal. That leaves our worth up to God too.

We can pray, *I don't feel very worthy. I've been told that I am special but I don't feel special. I feel terrible. Today it doesn't feel as if you love me. Help me believe that I am valuable.*

That simple directness places the foundation of our worth in God's hands. We believe we live in a world that we don't always understand, but it is a good world, and we believe that we are valuable.

This is the Divine Option.

6

Conscious
Commitment

If we're going to have a growing spiritual life that provides a foundation for self-worth, we have to decide we want it. As obvious as it sounds, we have to make a conscious commitment.

Commitment to anything doesn't happen because we think it's a good idea or because somebody suggested we ought to. Commitment requires decision, effort, and follow-through.

Conscious spiritual commitment can be compared to a desire for physical fitness. Most of us acknowledge that being fit is a good idea. That admission doesn't do anything to get us in shape. We must take decisive action.

After thinking about physical fitness for months, I took action in February 1976: I joined a health spa and followed the regimen my instructor laid out. I read and asked questions. I learned, among other things, that we need aerobic exercises requiring a steady use of oxygen for at least twenty minutes, three times a week, to benefit the cardiovascular system. Eventually I chose running.

When I started my program, the difficulty of running for even twenty minutes surprised—and exhausted—me. But I kept at it.

I soon understood why experts say that most people who start exercise programs seldom get past the second week. I hurt. My chest felt on fire. After a three-mile run I crumpled in exhaustion. But I persevered and it paid off. I currently run 30 to 35 miles a week.

Vern, a runner since 1984, went through his own discomfort and pain but he persisted. In late 1986 he completed his first marathon, 26.2 miles.

Becoming physically fit taught both of us the necessity of consciously committing ourselves to an exercise program. After years of sedentary living, Vern and I both had dozens of reasons to drop out. We had to make time in our already crowded schedules. We had to shift activities and priorities. We even gave up some social events.

My personal quest for physical fitness stemmed from a twofold motivation. First, I had reached the age of the bulging paunch, and my blood pressure was creeping up every year. (Both my parents suffered from high blood pressure.) Second was my conviction that the body is the temple of the Holy Spirit (see 1 Cor. 3:16–17; 6:19–20). Even more important, *my* body is God's temple.

This concept became a reality for me in 1976 while reading Romans 12:1: "I appeal to you therefore, brethren, by the mercies of God, to present your bodies as a living sacrifice, holy and acceptable to God, which is your spiritual worship." After being a Christian twenty years, two words in that verse impressed me as never before: *your bodies.*

Since that day I have strongly and consciously committed myself to having a healthy body. And the principles I use in that ongoing commitment also apply toward spiritual commitment. When we make this conscious commitment, we strive, among other things, to know ourselves better. Greater self-knowledge results in a healthier self-esteem.

Fitness Principles

When Vern and I compared physical to spiritual fitness, we came to several conclusions about their similarity.

1. Exercise doesn't feel good. This holds true in the beginning, at least. Almost everyone I talked to who started exercising after being sedentary said they had the same initial problem.

2. Keeping at it pays off. The first month was torture for Vern. He asked himself a hundred times, "Why am I doing this to myself?" Despite the question, he stuck with his program. Sometimes only the commitment to stick with it kept him going.

In the same way, through my own decision for ongoing spiritual growth, I have learned a lot about myself. At times I perceive personality aspects in myself I don't like. Facing such things hurts. We often don't want to know the torturous truths. At the same time, we know that if we stick with our conscious commitment to grow, eventually we benefit.

We learn to like ourselves more. Our faith in Jesus Christ enables us to continue growing. We see these new and exciting possibilities ahead. We also have the responsibility to work at making appropriate changes in our lives.

3. Pain eventually turns to pleasure. People who stick with running speak of the joy they regularly experience.

"I get a natural high," one runner said.

"I go out burdened with stress and problems and run for five miles, and I come back lighter, healthier, and relaxed," said another.

That concept of sticking with it taught Vern a lot in learning to love himself. He persisted even when he had to face unpleasant things in himself. He had to acknowledge his human limitations. The more he struggled with his feelings and stayed with them, the more he moved toward a healthy self-appreciation.

On the other hand, I once thought that if I could blot out my failures and know that I would not fail again, I could genuinely like myself. I had to learn that we don't love ourselves when we're perfect (we never are anyway!), and we don't love ourselves when we reach a particular level of achievement (we never reach a level high enough).

Beyond the Eraser Principle

I tried to use what Vern calls the Eraser Principle. I wanted to erase part of me—the part I called bad. The Eraser Principle says, "I will be acceptable when I get rid of all the bad parts of me." The Eraser Principle attacks every unacceptable feeling and attitude.

The Eraser Principle never erases enough because we can always see more bad to get rid of. Furthermore, it offers nothing positive. While the Eraser Principle attempts to take away the bad, it can never add anything good.

If we want to experience genuine self-love, we have to move beyond the Eraser Principle. We need to accept, appreciate, and validate everything about ourselves—the way we are right now.

For example, suppose I lost my temper several times recently. If I didn't like being angry, I labeled anger as bad. When I pasted on the label, I took upon myself a decision that is not mine to make. Although I could decry specific *acts* of anger in my life, to label anger in my life as bad usurps a role that belongs only to God. I would be claiming to know the difference between good and evil. In effect, I would be laying a new foundation for self-worth—my own knowledge.

Using labels to evaluate ourselves reminds me of a diagram of a steer in our family cookbook. It names and shows the location of every cut of beef, from the brisket to the flank. When we insist on deciding, judging, and labeling ourselves, it is as if we cut ourselves into forty segments and placed them on a table in piles of "Keep" and "Discard."

When we make these decisions, we have gone beyond our right. God labels the whole person as good. We are God's creation. Though we are sinful and often disobedient, we are not therefore evil. We are human—the apex of God's creation.

To judge, compartmentalize, or segment ourselves pushes us into a system of good (or godliness) different from God's. Although the immediate circumstances were different, Paul's warning to the Galatians is valid here. He opposed the efforts of teachers who wanted to establish a different basis of good and wrote to his converts in Galatia because this group, called Judaizers, was trying to subvert the plain teaching of the gospel.

These Judaizers believed in Jesus as the Savior and all the other things Paul taught. They wanted to add only one thing. They said, "If you want to follow Jesus Christ, you must obey the law of Moses and particularly the law of circumcision."

Paul would have none of it. He had proclaimed the gospel of

grace, and the people of Galatia had turned to God. He hammered away at the simple truth that we do nothing to earn the love of God. He wrote:

> I am astonished that you are so quickly deserting him who called you in the grace of Christ and turning to a different gospel—not that there is another gospel, but there are some who trouble you and want to pervert the gospel of Christ. But even if we, or an angel from heaven, should preach to you a gospel contrary to that which we preached to you, let him be accursed.
>
> (Galatians 1:6–8)

We can still confess our sins and bemoan our failures, but we must recognize that we cannot earn the love of God by ridding our lives of evil actions.

We also need to take another look at the way in which we try to do good. We spend our lives trying to be generous people. We do favors. We're involved in church and civic organizations. We're the first to volunteer and the last to go home. We want to earn high marks in God's kingdom. We make an equation like this:

Desire to be a good Christian +
continuous self-giving =
good Christian

Is that a correct equation?

Through honest probing, one day we admit that we're not doing these things from pure motives. We are bargaining, cutting deals to make us more acceptable to God and to our fellow humans. We end up making secret lists:

> I've cleaned the house five times; you could at least do the vacuuming.
>
> I've driven for the past four weeks; it's your turn to drive or else to pay for the gas.
>
> I'm always arranging parties to celebrate other workers' birthdays; now it's time for someone to set up a party for me.

What outwardly appeared as generosity turns out to have been an implied deal, a bargain.

This recognition gives us the opportunity to reexamine our evaluation of ourselves. Instead of making those determinations about good and bad, we need to learn to say, "My anger [or lust, or pride, or jealousy] involves part of my human emotion. I am going to learn how to channel or use it."

Otherwise, by calling a quality evil, I am saying, "This pride must not belong to me and I must separate myself from it because it is bad."

Commitment Factors

Our true starting place lies in seeing our human limitations. When that realization comes and we know we can never transcend our humanness, we make our conscious commitment to allow God to teach us. This commitment involves many factors, such as:

- a desire for a growing spiritual life
- a willingness to learn about our wholeness
- an openness to accept our darker side
- an opportunity to see what resides inside us without self-condemnation (see Rom. 8:1)

In short, we are committed to accepting ourselves as we are—as God accepts us.

This conscious commitment requires a rigorous introspection and a fearless honesty with ourselves. We can't do that without starting with the right understanding, an understanding that confesses, "I don't understand many things about myself. I do know I am lovable."

An Exercise in Self-Examination

We present ourselves to God and ask for help in our lifelong self-examination. Giving up prejudicial self-understanding sounds easier than it is. Here is an exercise to help us look inside ourselves.

1. On a sheet of paper, list adjectives describing all your positive traits—everything you can honestly say you like about yourself. Your list might start out like this:

gentle
compassionate
even-tempered

2. When you finish, write *I am* in front of each word:

I am gentle
I am compassionate
I am even-tempered

3. Make a list of the things you don't like about yourself, the traits you'd like to change:

selfish
talkative
lazy

3. As with the positive traits, write *I am* in front of each word.

I am selfish
I am talkative
I am lazy

These lists help us to see ourselves as whole beings. None of us is totally compassionate. No matter how loving we are, we can find traces of cruelty or indifference to needs we could meet.

Likewise, if we see ourselves as selfish, that is not a complete picture of ourselves. Even if we are aware of acting selfishly, we also recognize that at times we are self-giving, far beyond our duty or the expectation of those about whom we care deeply.

If we are rigorously honest we can find many sets of positive and negative traits within us. At first this discovery may produce a great deal of personal discomfort. Usually we are afraid to acknowledge the negative elements in our lives. We draw back from making statements such as:

I am petty-minded
I am jealous
I manipulate others to get approval
I try to control others to get my way

We think, Who would want to be around me if they knew I'm really this way? Actually, others *do* know we are this way. Or they would know if they observed us very much. All these opposing characteristics reside in us.

We can use our lists to get more in touch with ourselves. They will provide the raw data for our ongoing commitment to God.

Most of us need help in learning about ourselves. Many find therapy helpful. Others find guidance through the confessional. Others use support groups for just what the name says—support. How we use our lists is less important than the fact that we've made a conscious decision to follow through with self-examination. We have shown a willingness to learn more about who we are.

As we learn more about who we are, we can experience our wholeness more. When we experience more of a sense of wholeness, we have a greater sense of our value. We will love ourselves.

While I have called these lists "positive" and "negative," don't equate *positive* with *good* and *negative* with *bad*. We want to avoid deciding the good and the bad. We want, instead, to recognize who we are—a mixture. Let's not use this list to say, "Here's what's wrong with me." Instead we can say, "Here is a picture of who I am."

This requires a lot of courage and commitment. It also requires faith to admit, "I am trusting and I am doubtful. I am petty and I am generous."

Through prayer we present our list to God. One way of praying is to say, *God, I see that I am a petty and manipulative person. Help me be less destructive in the way I treat myself and others.* Do this with each of the negatives on the list.

Pray for an increase in those other qualities: *God, I am kind. Help me to be more kind and sensitive to the needs of those around me.*

We must remind ourselves that commitment never finishes. We're in the process of examining our motives and growing. As our lives change, we may find ourselves coming back to the same issue many times. Yet each time we come back on a different level.

For example, I grappled with the issue of anger during the early days after my conversion. I prayed a lot and God helped me. Anger no longer presented a problem. Twenty years later, I discovered anger again—on a different level. This time it lay below the surface. Instead of emerging like a volcanic explosion, it came out in subtle putdowns or through irritated remarks.

This time, instead of resorting to the Eraser Principle, I thought of anger as part of me. *God, I get angry. I don't like what I do when that happens. Help me with this problem.* I discovered several benefits from this approach:

> I acknowledge my ongoing need for God's help.
> I am more aware of my full self—both my positive side and my shadow side.
> I continue to dig deeper to discover the causes for my anger.
> I like myself more.

We never reach perfection. Someone said, "We're always practicing being perfect, but we never get enough practice." Our goal isn't perfection anyway. Our goal is the enduring commitment to stay in that gap where we are constantly struggling with what we can do vs. what we can't do.

As human beings we err on one side or the other. Either we try to do more than we can do or we abdicate responsibility. We want to keep exploring, to keep pushing inward. We ask ourselves, "Is there more I can do? Am I trying to fool myself into believing that I can do more?"

Let's see how this works out in a practical setting.

Carl has come home late for the third time without a phone call. His wife is angry. "You could at least call to say that you'll be late," she thunders at him.

Carl says to himself, Something must be going on inside me. Ellen's right. I'm not even being courteous.

He digs deeper and finally admits that he is angry with Ellen. He didn't like several remarks she made to him three weeks ago. On an unconscious level, Carl has found a way to teach her a lesson for being unkind.

After serious introspection and honesty he understands. He finally realizes that he's been manipulative and deceptive in the way he has handled himself. Now he can do something different.

Carl doesn't call himself *bad* for his attitude and subsequent action. He's not bad, he only handled his feelings in an unloving way.

He does not need to say, "I'm evil and worthless. I'm sneaky in the way I get back at my wife." He admits, "Yes, I did that, but it isn't how I want to be." Carl is moving ahead in his growth, toward a healthier sense of self-love.

He still needs to learn to express his feelings in a more constructive way. Nonetheless, he's learned a valuable lesson, and it increases his commitment to grow.

7

Taking
Responsibility

"You make me angry."
"My father ruined my life."
"My husband won't let me."
We've all heard these statements and others like them. None of those making them take responsibility for their own actions. The first speaker, for example, won't acknowledge anger from inside himself. He blames someone else.

If we grow toward loving ourselves, we have to learn to accept responsibility for our feelings and for our actions. Rather than deal with our unwillingness to do so, we make excuses and we blame others.

We can see this in chapter 5 of John's Gospel. A man who lay at the pool of Beth-zatha received healing from Jesus. Until that time he had never assumed responsibility for anything. He had been ill for thirty-eight years. Friends had made a pallet for him to lie on while he waited for the special times when, as the folklore had it, the waters bubbled and the first person into the water received healing.

Jesus stopped in front of the crippled man and asked him a simple question: "Do you want to be healed?"

The sick man never answered that question; he made an excuse. "Sir, I have no man to put me into the pool when the water is troubled, and while I am going another steps down before me" (John 5:7).

We don't know if he replied in an angry tone, as if to say, You stupid fool, why do you think I've been here for so long? What a question! Of course I want to be healed.

He may have been saying, Lord, you don't know how long I've suffered by this pool. I'm so tired of coming day after day and getting passed by.

No matter what he meant or whether he said it angrily, self-pityingly, or stoically, he didn't answer *directly.* He never accepted responsibility for wanting to be healed.

Taking responsibility does not mean that we can heal ourselves. It doesn't mean that we can climb down into the waters unaided. Taking responsibility speaks initially of a desire. We do what we can. Just that willingness can greatly empower us.

Jesus' question itself could have empowered the sick man. I suspect that he had lain there on his pallet for so many years he lost any concept of having a choice.

For us, each time we take responsibility, even in little things, we make life easier for ourselves. Otherwise our lives can become so chaotic that the only thing we have power over is whether we will wash our dishes today.

It's easy to say, "My life is such a mess. It isn't worth fighting anymore." We all find times when we want to give up. We don't have any energy left to battle it out.

Yet there's always something we can do. It may be pitifully small, but we gain strength by doing even that much. It may be a tiny fragment of all the things that must be done, but it is a beginning. Giving up says we're taking the easier, less painful way instead of assuming responsibility.

Of course, the opposite approach is the grandiose system of belief that boasts, "Anything my mind can conceive and believe, I can achieve." We can never accomplish everything we attempt. Such an attitude makes us feel defeated when we fail.

Either way we fail to take responsibility for who we are—and that includes an honest appraisal of our abilities and inabilities.

Six Responsible Steps

We don't know everything about ourselves and probably never will. We can take responsibility for what we can accomplish. These steps lead to a fuller life and a recognition of our lovability. Here are six ways in which we need to take responsibility.

1. We need to take responsibility for our disappointments.
Many times when we serve others we expect reciprocity without specifically saying it. When the other does not respond by doing something for us or giving us what we want, we feel keenly disappointed.

Even if our attitude is, "I'll do nine things for you and I only want one back," we are making deals instead of giving gifts.

2. We need to take responsibility for our self-deceptions. We sometimes call them blind spots. Haven't we all known people like Ann, who fell wildly in love with Jack? Friends tried to tell her the truth about him, but she wouldn't listen. Even when she had evidence, she refused to accept it. Later, she discovered Jack's true nature.

"He deceived me," she wails. Perhaps. But part of it involved Ann's willingness to deceive herself. She didn't want to know.

That's the key to self-deception—we don't want to know. To reverse that means we are working at being honest with ourselves about ourselves. It may not be easy to do, but it's important for us to take responsibility to engage in this effort.

For those of us who want to be more congruous, we need to expose our self-deceptions. When we are honest with ourselves we are freer to love and more capable of loving. Otherwise we relate to others as if they are objects and not people. We attempt to manipulate them into what we believe they ought to be.

3. We need to take responsibility for our failures. Failures teach us about our humanness and remind us that we are not God. We can direct our energies into what we can control instead of what we can't.

One woman said, "Some days I'm acutely disappointed in my husband's distance. I get sick of my adolescent children's rebellion. I have no control over these areas."

In many ways she doesn't. Yet when she acknowledges that she doesn't have control, that she can't run the world the way it ought to be, she can focus on the things she *can* do. She finally said, "Some days the only thing I know I can be in charge of is whether or not I make the beds. But when I'm all tied up in trying to make my husband and daughter turn out like they should, I don't even do the beds."

4. We have to accept responsibility for accepting the world as it is. Many areas won't change for us, and they defy our control. We readily see what's wrong with others. We can want them to change, beg them to change, and offer to help them to do things differently. But we can't force them. When we acknowledge the world as it is, we start to separate what we can be responsible for and what we can't. That also helps us in learning to love ourselves because we are seeing ourselves as we are.

This concept reminds me of the serenity prayer by Reinhold Niebuhr, as adapted by Alcoholics Anonymous:

> God grant me the serenity to accept the things
>   I cannot change,
> courage to change the things I can,
> and wisdom to know the difference.

We can't always be in charge. We're not God. Although we don't seek pain and loss, when these adverse times come into our lives they don't have to be our enemies. They can teach us and thereby turn out to be constructive.

5. We have to take responsibility for our own suffering. When I use the word "suffering," I refer to the seemingly bad things that happen to us over which we have no control.

We don't seek suffering, yet we should not automatically reject problems, pain, hardships, setbacks, and difficulties. We have no way of knowing in advance the ultimate meaning of seeming tragedy. Whether fair or not, it is our suffering and we have to learn to cope with it.

For example, I had known Sara for years. We lost touch, and when we were reacquainted recently, I learned that her older daughter had died in a traffic accident. I told her how sorry I was.

"It was a terrible time for us," Sara said. "We went through a lot of pain for a couple of years. But out of that, I've learned how to help others face their losses and tragedies. Until we lost our daughter, I'd always lived one of those seemingly charmed lives."

Her husband said, "One day we were talking, wondering how we could ever live a normal life again. I was so depressed and upset, I was ready to call off our marriage. I told a friend. She asked me only one question. 'What are you learning from all this tragedy?' I hadn't asked that question before."

They soon took responsibility for their suffering: that is, they accepted it as unchangeable and decided to live *and grow* from the experience.

Luke 9:51 describes the great moment of responsibility in the life of Jesus. He knew his purpose in life. His destiny lay in Jerusalem. "When the days drew near for him to be received up, he set his face to go to Jerusalem."

To go to Jerusalem meant torture, betrayal, and death. He decided to go anyway. Had he rejected suffering he wouldn't have gone on.

The book of Hebrews rallies suffering believers to look beyond their persecution and torment by referring to Jesus' decision to suffer.

> Let us fix our eyes on Jesus, the author and perfecter of our faith, who for the joy set before him endured the cross, scorning its shame, and sat down at the right hand of the throne of God. Consider him who endured such opposition from sinful men, so that you will not grow weary and lose heart. (Hebrews 12:2–3, NIV)

Jesus went to Jerusalem and to his own death. He went with the faith that God would make something good come out of rejection, pain, and suffering. Ironically, believing in the midst of crucifixion that good will come exhibits the ultimate faith.

At times we symbolically identify with Jesus. Most of us have known times when we felt as if we had entered the grave for two or three days. We despaired. Everything had fallen apart—death of a loved one, loss of a job, chronic illness. We slowly came out of the grave, and our faith enabled us to trust in new life for us. Yet we don't experience that kind of faith until we experience "death" in the form of despair or discouragement.

The experiences we call painful, evil, or bad turn out to be necessary ingredients for our growth.

6. We have to take responsibility for being flawed. A big step in the development of self-esteem comes when, like all other human creatures, we grasp that no matter how hard we work, we are and always will be imperfect. When we accept our own imperfections, we have more self-compassion. We also grow more tolerant of other people's imperfections. We allow more room for acceptance, understanding, and forgiveness.

We live in an imperfect world and with people who are never all we want them to be. Our parents disappoint us. Our spouses and friends fail. Instead of spending vast energy trying to make them perfect or resenting them for not being everything we need, we are free to make decisions about how we want to handle our situation.

Most of us expected a certain amount of nurture from our family. Most of us also ended up disappointed with the amount or the quality of the nurture we received. While we wanted more, we received only partial satisfaction.

We coped and we wondered, What's wrong with me? What's wrong with my parents? We blame the people we expected to love us and ask, What's wrong with them that they don't give me love when I need it so badly?

Implied in these situations is the feeling that emptiness, rejection, and loneliness should not be ours. Or we naively assume that we can learn a magic process to remove them. If we take responsibility for our whole selves, however, we acknowledge (and actually claim) our own emptiness.

Once we understand the reality of human imperfection in all of us, we recognize that we can't change circumstances. But we can change our questions. If a particular relationship is not fulfilling, where else can I get my needs met? No one person can supply everything I want out of friendship, so how do I go about making additional friends? Do I want to maintain this relationship in which I feel so much pain and rejection?

We look more clearly at ourselves and at the people involved in our lives. We stop holding their flaws against them. We can even learn to laugh a little more and say, "We're flawed and they're flawed."

Going to the Well

Vern likes to use the analogy of the old-fashioned well. We take our water bucket and go daily to the well. One day, however, we drop our bucket down and it comes up empty. We try again, but still no water. No matter how often we drop that bucket into the well, we get the same result. At that point, we have choices.

1. We never give up. We say, "I'm going to drop my bucket down the well until I finally bring water up." We're working desperately for something we can't have.

2. We curse the well. We scream, "What's wrong with you? I came here before and you gave me water. You have no right to stop now. It isn't fair. You certainly don't behave like the well I started with. You have totally failed me."

3. We wonder if our technique is wrong. Is something wrong with me? I got water before. What's wrong with me that I can't get it any more?

4. Perhaps we've never gotten water out of that well. We wonder, What would it be like if I could pull up a bucket of that sweet water? Wouldn't I feel refreshed by it? Why can't I have it? Other people have gotten it.

5. We stay at the well, yearning for it to provide nourishing water once again. In the meantime, we remain thirsty. Eventually we turn resentful. As that resentment grows, we might destroy the well.

6. We accept the fact that the well has run dry and look for alternative sources of water. We may never understand the reason. The well simply doesn't have water to give to us. Whatever the cause, we take responsibility for taking care of ourselves.

In applying the analogy of the well, we can examine ourselves. Some of us had affection in childhood but never enough. Now we want "enough" and can't have it. Others of us never had a parent, or any parental affection, and spend our lives wondering what it would have been like with a real mother.

Whether we've ever gotten anything out of the well is almost beside the point if we continue to insist that we ought to get something. In our lives there's just no question of whether we're going to be hurt and disappointed. The real question is, How often?

There's also no question of whether we're going to hurt somebody else. Again, it's how often?

When we can take responsibility for the fact that we will never be perfectly fed, nor can we perfectly feed, we admit our human limitations. We free our energies to seek whatever sustenance we can find instead of wasting our strength seeking what we can't have.

Taking responsibility requires a clear look at our wants and our expectations in light of reality. Can we satisfy them or not?

At some time in our adult life we need to accept our parents as they are—ordinary people who probably gave us what they could, sometimes not even that. One thing is clear, however. Nobody gets loved enough, not even those with the most consistently loving parents in the world.

Once we understand that there is nothing wrong with us because we didn't get enough love, we can also accept the reality that there's nothing wrong with others because they didn't give enough. They share the same limitations. Once we admit this, we can accept the responsibility to provide for our own nurture.

That search for fulfillment for our needs is often a lonely journey. Yet it's a freeing experience because we are not bound to the past, constantly demanding satisfaction from the empty well. There's a kind of harmony with reality that at least makes us more efficient in our living. We don't expend so much fruitless effort.

Admitting our needs makes us less critical of other people for their humanity. We can acknowledge that they are limited too. We live in an imperfect world. We can put ourselves in a position to receive more, but we also develop a willingness to accept that sometimes we're just going to go empty.

Every human being is partially empty and always needy. In TV sitcoms all families laugh and love together. Our neighbors appear happy. We compare them with our own family life and lose in the comparison.

What is wrong with us? With me? What is wrong with my parents? My spouse? Instead of thinking, That's how the world is, we accept the illusion that everybody else is fine but we're not. And that *is* an illusion. Can we expect life to imitate TV sitcoms, which resolve every crisis in thirty minutes?

The sense of emptiness makes us feel that somebody has failed. When we hold that attitude we may attack somebody else for not being perfect, or we may turn the guilt onto ourselves. If we could figure out how to get fixed up, we could be perfect.

Vern sometimes shows clients a little sign he keeps in his office:

> Our sense of failure depends on
> our need to be perfect.

As long as we need to be perfect, to be good to be loved, we will always fail. We can't be perfect and we'll always feel inadequate. We create our own failure.

The need to be perfect is, in reality, a need to be irresponsible. It shows our unwillingness to be responsible for our flaws. We treat imperfections as enemies.

This is not to say we shouldn't work toward improving ourselves. We're obligated to be all that we can be, even though none of us can be everything. When we try to be everything or to do everything exactly right, we are seeking omnipotence. If we go the other way and say, "Since I'm imperfect, I'm nothing," that's equally irresponsible.

For example, Ed wants to be more loving. He tries to tell his wife things he doesn't like about her and their relationship. But he crosses the line from saying "I don't like what's going on" to communicate a very different message: "You ought to change."

As soon as he goes beyond admitting his discomfort and demands that she change, he tries to control her. In effect, he is saying, You are unacceptable to me unless you meet these conditions.

We're always in process. We're always going to make mistakes. That's part of our human condition. When we acknowledge that, we can rectify what we're able to change. But if we believe it's against the rules to make mistakes, we have difficulty in changing. We spend energy trying to hide our flaws or concentrate on putting ourselves down when we're trying to improve.

Many self-improvement courses start with the assumption that we're not OK people. They imply that we have to improve in order to be OK.

This is different from the biblical position. We are acceptable to God. Right now. We all have areas where we need to improve. We all need to be more loving, more sensitive, more faithful.

Yet having needs doesn't make us unacceptable. That's also where many of us stumble. We find it hard to believe that we are

acceptable to God *right now,* just as we are. That's God's grace.
I can't explain God's grace. I can't explain God's love. I certainly can't attempt to comprehend *why* God loves us.

I can do only one thing: *accept it.*

When I understand that God loves me, knowing all my imperfections—things I haven't even acknowledged yet—it tells me a wonderful truth. When I know God loves me, I am responseable—able to respond and to be responsible.

Exercise

Here are three examples of well-known people whose attitude toward personal tragedy became redemptive and provided an opportunity for growth.

Eleanor Roosevelt, who stood in the shadow of four-time President Franklin D. Roosevelt, emerged as first lady of the world in the years following her husband's death.

Helen Keller, because of an illness at nineteen months, was deaf, blind, and almost mute. Yet this woman graduated with honors from Radcliffe College, wrote five books, and brought the plight of the blind and deaf to the world's attention.

Candy Lightner, after her teenage daughter was killed by a drunken driver, formed Mothers Against Drunk Driving—MADD—in 1980. Through her efforts, several states have passed more severe legislation against those who drive under the influence of alcohol.

Recall the words of the apostle Paul:

> Praise be to the God and Father of our Lord Jesus Christ, the Father of compassion and the God of all comfort, who comforts us in all our troubles, so that we can comfort those in any trouble with the comfort we ourselves have received from God.
>
> (2 Corinthians 1:3–4, NIV)

Review your life. On paper list three to five "bad" things that have happened in your life for which you have seen yourself as victimized and helpless. With the perspective of time, have any of these events been opportunities that could not be seen at the time they occurred?

8

Self-Disclosure

I have a friend who has always abhorred violence in any form. He served in the Korean conflict but made it clear that it would not be in a combatant status.

"I believe in defending my country," he said, "but I could not kill another human being regardless of the circumstances."

In the fall of 1986 he saw *Extremities* with Farrah Fawcett and James Russo. In the film, Russo attempts to rape Miss Fawcett but she escapes. She reports the incident to the police. They tell her, "Even if we caught him, it would just be his word against yours."

Russo has her wallet with her address in it. A week later he comes to her house with the intention of raping and then killing her. He overpowers Fawcett but she manages to escape and turn the tables on him. She thinks of calling the police but Russo reminds her, "It's just your word against mine."

Fawcett ties him up and decides to kill him. Her two roommates come home and argue with her against killing her assailant.

My friend said, "I found myself growing intensely angry at the violence of that man. I also realized that if I had been in the place of the female victim, I could have killed him."

The film enabled him to grasp a new side of himself. All his life he had believed himself incapable of violence. Finally he knew he had that capacity.

Once he realized this about himself, he told a few people he trusted. He expected them to react with shock, even disgust. They didn't. One of them said, "How nice to see the human side of you."

Each of those to whom he disclosed this part of himself valued him more as a person. Their acceptance enabled him to say, "This is part of me. I am capable of love and compassion. I'm also a man capable of violence."

Strange as it may sound, understanding this aspect of his personality enabled him to love himself more. "I see myself as more of a whole person. I'm not just a man trying to live in narrow obedience to God. I'm also a man whose obedience leads him to discover and acknowledge a wide range of feelings, including rage."

He learned a valuable lesson about self-disclosure. He learned what many of us still do not grasp: disclosing ourselves enables us to love ourselves more. Although that may seem contradictory, self-disclosure opens the way for us to have a clearer understanding of who we are. As we learn who we are, we accept ourselves with all our imperfections.

Self-disclosure forms an integral part of learning to love ourselves. This self-revealing involves a commitment to learn about ourselves. Two significant things grow out of this. First, when we disclose ourselves to other people whom we trust, their acceptance helps us realize that we are not bad or evil, only human and flawed. Second, self-understanding implies acting on what we have learned.

By taking responsibility for who he is, my friend now saw himself differently. Although aware of his capacity for violence, he did not start lashing out in blind rage. He didn't excuse himself for getting angry. He said, "Once I admitted this potential for violence, I felt more compassionate toward hostile, vitriolic people. Before that, I used to think that if they wanted to calm down their angry natures they could do it. They only needed a little more self-control. That was before I found myself aroused so easily."

Until we search ourselves, it's also impossible for us to let anybody know who we are. What we don't know, we can't disclose. To love and be loved involves two steps: self-disclosure and acceptance.

If we choose only one or the other of these steps, we won't feel loved. We can reveal ourselves, but it doesn't guarantee that others will love us. We could frighten, disgust, or antagonize them. By seeking acceptance without self-disclosure, people can accept us but we don't feel loved by them. For instance, I may not have been honest in what I've let others know about myself. When they express acceptance, inwardly I'm saying, "Yes, but—" and dismissing their words. We need both steps for self-love to occur.

In group situations, once participants feel at ease with each other and develop some trust, they usually candidly reveal parts of their hidden selves.

In all the group work in which I've been involved, when an individual risked self-disclosure, the others accepted the revelation and the person as well. There were comments such as, "Thanks for telling us that. Now I know you a little better."

Growing in self-love also involves accepting our own incompleteness. We live with a willingness to reexamine the old ways of thinking and acting. Many of these old ways get in the way of our learning about ourselves and taking responsibility for who we are.

Only when we take responsibility for being who we are *right now* can we do something about changing. If we blame parents, school, society, friends, or mates, we don't change. If the cause lies elsewhere, why should we work at changing?

We not only have to admit responsibility and be open to new understanding, but also allow God to help us. Self-examination opens the way for God to teach us and lead us in new directions.

We can't predict what will come out of our experiences when we reveal ourselves. Not knowing what will happen may scare us. My experience and that of others confirms that as we know more about ourselves, we love the new us more because the new us will be a more complete individual.

In religious circles many of us learned the rule that we must love God first, others second, and ourselves third. This triad implied that we loved God and others through a rigorous, fearless, self-giving, self-denying stance. After we had done everything we could for God and our neighbors, we could do something for ourselves. We believed that we should ignore ourselves because caring for self interfered with serving God and others.

In reality, it works the other way. As we love ourselves, we become more self-knowledgeable and more self-accepting. That gives us greater impetus to serve God and others. Unfortunately, many still identify self-love with selfishness. "You have to get your mind off yourself," they tell us.

Do we ever get our minds off ourselves? I know that until we have a healthy self-respect we constantly think about ourselves in an unhealthy manner.

> How will others react to us?
> What will they think of us?
> How can we be as good/kind/successful?
> What can we do to make them like us better?

Once we like who we are, we lose our compulsiveness to compare ourselves with others. We also make a commitment to live in God's creation as it is, not as we wish it to be. This leads us into rethinking ourselves, our values, and our goals.

Five Steps in Self-Understanding

When we move toward self-love, most of us go through a process in self-understanding. We move through five steps as we look honestly at ourselves.

1. I'm a bad person. Recognition starts as we become aware of a particular character trait that we consider bad, wicked, or evil. When we recognize in ourselves selfishness, bad temper, or laziness, for example, we naturally consider ourselves to be selfish, bad-tempered, or lazy as if one aspect of us becomes the whole. "How could anyone love me if I'm really this way?"

Initially we can't think of our mistakes, shortcomings, and failures as things we do. We tend to think of them in terms of who we are.

We confuse our behavior with our selves. Because we have done a certain act (or have done it habitually), we assume we are a certain kind of person.

2. I do bad things. To say "I am an angry person" is not the same as saying, "I am angry," or "I feel angry now." The first statement describes the person. The second and third describe a quality or action.

A wise friend once said, "You failed in one thing. Failure doesn't make *you* anything." Another time he talked with a distraught woman who had recently gone through a divorce—the first in her family. He said, "You failed in one aspect of your life. Your life is not a failure."

3. *I'm vulnerable.* We have to be able to hurt a little if necessary. We become vulnerable and risk sharing our pain with someone else. We wonder, What if they reject me?

Most of us don't want to be frauds. We don't want to live a lie. Yet sometimes we experience fear and worry about possible rejection if we make ourselves known.

We're hesitant to risk showing our shadow side, as Carl Jung called it. It's easier to hide behind masks, rules, games, and defined roles. It may be initially painful to expose our nakedness to others. To reveal ourselves openly takes a lot of courage. But we can do it! If we want to love ourselves, we *will* do it.

At that stage of vulnerability, we have no assurance of how others will respond to our honest confession. Yet if we're determined to know ourselves and to love ourselves, this is something we can't bypass.

4. *I'm human.* We accept our flaws. We join with all other human beings. We grasp that we're not greatly different from others.

I have discovered that disclosing something about myself to another person—especially something I have felt ashamed about—makes me a more rounded human being.

During seminary days my homiletics professor once said, "We can't separate ourselves from the biblical text. When we apply truths to the congregation, the same truths apply to us." In my first sermons I tried to apply the message of the biblical text and the problems to myself as well as to the congregation. When I preached on anger, I included an incident in my life when I battled the matter of losing my temper—and lost.

After my third Sunday, the church organist told me, "I like having a human being in the pulpit. I make a lot of mistakes, and it helps me to know that you do too."

The more I thought about this, the more I started to analyze sermons by other preachers. Most of them either avoided personal references or told only stories that subtly illustrated their integrity, superior wit, or courageous stand for their faith. Such sermons never allowed listeners to know the real person in the pulpit.

5. *I'm understood.* It comforts us to hear the genuine response, "I understand." We are known as we are. Once we are known, we are loved.

That quality of understanding reminds me of a large North Carolina church that was holding lay renewal meetings. Eighteen lay people spoke at various informal and formal worship services. The leader scheduled two lay people to give a brief testimony on the closing night of what brought them to their faith in Jesus Christ.

The two selected to speak—unknown to each other—had been sexually abused as children. The first, a woman, spoke briefly of her experience and added that only after she had come into the church had she found love and inner healing through others. The second, a man, had been sexually abused by his mother. He stood up to speak and tears filled his eyes. He had to fight for control of his emotions so that he could tell his story. "For the first time in my life, I have found people that I know can understand . . . and can love me. I've thought of myself as unclean and unlovable."

He concluded by saying, "For a lot of years, I've felt like an alien on planet earth. Now I know that I am truly an earthling."

Our Flawed Selves

These five steps show us that we can start with a willingness to learn more about who we are and share that knowledge without judging ourselves as bad. We suspend our self-criticism and allow God to decide. God has already announced forgiveness and mercy, reminding us that God never rejects us.

Without confidence in God's concern for us and the loving security we discover in others, we feel ourselves acceptable only when we do well or please others. For instance, it's a painful discovery to realize that all of us hate. More accurately, that *I* hate. That I am capable of physical destruction. Most of us shy away from admitting that we would be capable of murderous thoughts. Yet if we are ruthlessly honest with ourselves, we admit that we have felt such feelings.

I wonder if we recognize the words of violence in the familiar words of the lullaby, "Down will come cradle, baby and all." That's not exactly a loving wish for an infant. These words express a reservoir of ambivalence that we feel for some of our dearest, most innocent children of God.

If we are ruthlessly honest we also acknowledge the mix of jealousy and competition in our friendships. If a co-worker doesn't get her promotion, we wouldn't wish for her failure but we're not sorry she didn't get it.

It's impossible to be married without sometimes having hostile feelings for the spouse. Any two people in a loving relationship at times experience hateful feelings toward each other.

Vern recalls that his mentor in therapy used to ask couples, "Have you thought about killing your spouse?"

This usually evoked shock and an emphatic "No."

"Oh, my goodness," he would answer. "This is going to take a long time."

He believed that the willingness to acknowledge our negative feelings plays a vital part in allowing love to win over hate. He knew that ambivalence is a part of all human relationships. We want to determine for ourselves what is good and won't allow ourselves to feel such negative feelings—or to admit it if we do. For us to have feelings we label bad makes us bad people.

If we can learn to say, "This is who I am. I'm an uneven mixture of contradictory feelings, many of them not pretty," we can also learn to ask, "How can I use these feelings?" Instead of trying to erase parts of ourselves, we will try to use all that we have been given. That process may sound odd, but it's part of what we have to go through in order to move along the path to true self-love. We all have negative feelings. We can turn them around and make them positive if we're willing.

One friend said, "If we weren't aggressive we wouldn't have the potential for destruction. Out of the same emotion of aggressiveness comes the ability to be assertive."

We begin to learn to rechannel such negative feelings as aggressiveness when we acknowledge them. When we don't acknowledge them, we have to spend enormous energy restraining them. If we don't hold them back, they run rampant. Or they come out in subtle ways. One therapist says, "We leak around the edges." He explained that since we can't, for instance, acknowledge anger, we smile warmly but our words have a bite to them. When someone reacts offensively to a statement, we apologize profusely: "I didn't mean it that way." But we really did mean it, and we don't like being found out.

Even with the most rigorous control, these negative emotions sometimes build up inside. When the pressure reaches a certain level, we erupt anyway. We virtually lose control until the eruption ceases. Then we galvanize our resources to gain control again. We become like volcanoes—and no one knows when the next eruption will occur.

Once we acknowledge our negative side and freely disclose it to others, we learn a valuable lesson. We learn to trust that all of us—every part—is valuable. We're not valuable only when we perform like everybody else. We're as valuable in our anger or aggressiveness (even though we don't condone the behavior) as we are when we are cooperative and gentle.

Another important part of self-disclosure is that we cannot be loved unless we're known. We will always be saying secretly, if not out loud, "You wouldn't like me if you really knew what I was thinking." Or, "If you knew what I'm really like, you'd turn away from me."

When we can trust in God's acceptance of us, we can accept ourselves. That leads us toward entrusting ourselves to other people. When we experience that level of trust, we open the possibility for true intimacy.

The movement toward intimacy includes self-disclosure. Oddly enough, the primary beneficiary of that openness is ourselves. We no longer have to use our energies to hide the "shameful truths" about ourselves.

All of us have parts of ourselves that are private. We also have the right to our own secrets. I'm not talking about an obligatory openness where we *must* disclose everything to others. In the 1960s groups sprang up in search of helping people find intimacy and selfhood. They wanted to get in touch with their "real selves." In their methods, they forced participants to disclose themselves. They vied for who could open up the fastest and overwhelm the group with the deepest secret. Some of those participants left feeling contempt for themselves and confused about their experience. They weren't ready to bare their souls. They had no assurance that the others would keep their secrets inviolate.

The Garden of Eden story illustrates this fear of disclosure. Adam and Eve knew they had disobeyed. They were afraid. They saw themselves as bad and broke the relationship with God. They had disappointed God and God may even have been angry, but they broke the intimacy. They hid from God and they tried to cover it up by making clothes for themselves out of fig leaves. (I am using anthropomorphic language, in the spirit of the biblical story.)

Sad to say, they never regained the intimacy they had previously experienced with God. They did not acknowledge their failure. Adam blamed Eve. By inference, he also blamed God for giving him that woman. She blamed the serpent.

They broke the relationship because they decided that disobedience made them unacceptable. That kind of self-definition doesn't allow for the possibility that God can be both angry and loving toward us. It upsets God when any of the human creation break the relationship.

I sometimes wonder how the Garden story would have ended if Adam and Eve had said, "Yes, we disobeyed. We realize that, in our greed to be like you, we played into the hands of the serpent."

They would have understood themselves better. They could have faced their imperfection and aloneness. They might have liked themselves a lot better.

The same is true with us.

9

Our Lonely Selves

After ten action-filled, people-involving years as a pastor of a growing congregation I resigned. I had been writing as a sideline for a long time, and in 1984 I became a full-time writer.

That's when I discovered loneliness.

Loneliness had been with me all along, just below the surface. I refused to give it much attention. I was heavily involved with people, activities, and ideas. I avoided confronting loneliness. I made uneasy truces and forced my loneliness into dormancy for a long time before it worked its way into the foreground of my life.

Then everything changed for me. I found myself sitting in an upstairs bedroom converted into an office. I seldom had visitors and few telephone calls. For hours each day I sat in front of my word processor and wrote. By the end of the third week, the face of loneliness had started to come to me regularly.

I have since adjusted to being alone and to the feeling of aloneness. I still write every day, allowing few interruptions. My friends know that my being home during the day does not mean I'm available for social visits. If more than two or three phone calls interrupt my solitude, I turn on the answering machine.

Some days I wish the phone would ring or that friends would drop in. I want to hear another human voice or to seek a diversion. I also accept that as part of loneliness.

I've learned a few things about loneliness through the sheer experience of living through it. At one time I saw loneliness as an enemy. Now I embrace it as a friend.

Normalcy of Loneliness

A film shown on TV was called *Lonely Are the Brave.* Yes, I thought, and so are the cowards, and the strong, and the weak, and everybody else. A characteristic of human life is being lonely. It touches us in every part of our lives.

If we can allow ourselves to be sensitive to our deeper needs, we discover this human struggle to understand ourselves and move beyond our estrangement. Yet we never complete the task. It's part of the human journey.

Here are a few of the things I've learned about loneliness and how it has helped me to love myself more fully.

1. Loneliness reminds us of our incompleteness. Loneliness grows out of our inner pain. it originates in our alienation from God and our separateness from other human creatures. At times we feel different and isolated from others. None of us ever reaches total wholeness. We always realize a piece of us is missing. That may be the one major quality that prevents us from being divine.

Yet most of us go to any length to deny this incompleteness. We marry. We work harder. We go back to school. We find a variety of ways to hide from ourselves. We'll keep finding those ways until something happens that forces us to gaze inwardly.

Many of us join support groups of various kinds. We genuinely want to reach others and to be reached. We seek to know the truth about ourselves. Instinctively we feel we can do this successfully through sharing ourselves.

We're searching for answers locked up inside ourselves. We need those who can probe and view us with objectivity.

I have one friend who has a talent to force me to think deeply for the answers within. He is superb at helping people like me move into contemplative moods. He suggests no answers and often doesn't know them anyway. He constantly reminds us, "Deep inside, you already know. Just keep prying into yourself." He's been right every time with me.

Even with his help, I may not arrive at solutions in his presence.

More than once he has probed into dark and murky parts of me and said, "Think about it. It'll come to you."

He knows—and I have confirmed—that some answers come to us only in the midst of solitude. We understand only as we go through those times of isolation from other people. They are answers no one else can give. We have to discover them for ourselves through the painful scrutinizing of our motives, desires, needs, hopes, and a hundred other factors.

2. *Loneliness motivates us to seek a cure.* Loneliness feels uncomfortable. Sometimes it's like a throbbing pain that won't go away. We feel different from others, as if no one else in the universe experiences loneliness quite the way we do.

Because we don't want to accept our loneliness, we work at not being lonely. The marriage-divorce-remarriage cycle may reflect this need. Live-in lovers move out, to be replaced almost immediately.

"Anything's better than living alone," a three-time divorcée told me.

Because it hurts so much, we know there must be a cure for loneliness and we determine to find it. We never do. We can become less lonely. We can learn to appreciate loneliness. But as long as we perceive loneliness as a disease from which we must find healing, we never get beyond the agony.

3. *Loneliness is a yearning for intimacy.* Many of us are of two minds about closeness to others. We long for closeness, to ease the misery of loneliness, yet we fear it. We like the *idea* of intimacy, although we may stiffen at a human touch or embrace.

In our search for intimacy we face the illusion of romantic love—the search for one special person in life who makes us whole. Yet no person can do that for us.

My friend Jerry essentially said that to me. He went through a marital breakup and a serious love affair shortly before we met. He learned one special thing from his pain. "I always looked for a woman to provide for every need I had. Now I know nobody can do that for me."

Jerry is dating cautiously again. "But now I know I have to find my own solutions. Other people can't give me everything I want no matter how hard they try. Or how hard I try to make them."

I once had the idea that marriage to the right wife plus having one or two special friends would give me all the intimacy I needed. It took me a long time to grasp the fallacy of that thinking. No two or three people could gratify all my needs.

As good as the relationship is with my wife, we both experience our moments of isolation. Friendships help provide what our primary love relationship lacks. But no matter how many friends we have, we still never have all the intimacy we desire.

We make our connections with other human beings. We share special moments together. But every moment isn't special. The intensity level varies. We don't want to give up or lose our special friends, but loneliness helps us recognize their proper place in our existence.

Friends accept us as we are. For our moments together they allow us to be ourselves. They enhance our self-esteem because they think we're OK the way we are and allow us to be that way.

In reflective moments, most of us admit we want a deeper kind of life. We long to find a place or a person who helps us recognize the true inner us, who helps us to respond to our own possibilities as well as to the realities beyond us of which loneliness makes us aware. We yearn for a friend who knows everything about us, understands everything, and meets any need we bring to the relationship. Unfortunately, no person can ever measure up to those demands. George Santayana said it this way: "People are friends in spots."

People can be friends only in selected areas; no one can contribute to us all that we need. We share only so much with each other. No one knows the whole us, or could. Sometimes we feel lonely because there is the *me* nobody knows. In our loneliness, we confront that unknown *me.*

4. Loneliness can turn us to God. Loneliness is a consequence of what is wrong about human beings. Some call it being off-center, egocentric. Biblically we call it fallen. Theologically we say that sin separates us from God. Our innate sinful natures tell us that we never overcome that barrier.

From that sense of aloneness we can turn toward God. When we reach the real depths of despair, don't we instinctively turn to God? Out of World War II came the saying, "There are no atheists in foxholes." The anguish of fear (which is also a part of loneliness) drives us beyond ourselves.

Our hunger for God is an acknowledgment of human estrangement. Some of us try everything else and conclude that ultimate
intimacy and oneness comes in our relatedness to our God.
Augustine said, "Our souls are restless until they find their rest
in thee."

My own conversion started after an ill-fated love affair. She
rejected me, and in my pain I began asking the basic questions:
Is this all there is to life? We live, we die, and have ups and downs
in between; isn't there something more?

A self-proclaimed agnostic, I had not been inside a church for
ten years. Then an unexplainable something led me toward a
chapel one night, and I went inside. The room, lit only by a single
recessed light, gave me a sense of privacy and deepened my
loneliness. I sat in a pew. I didn't know how to pray and had no
faith that God existed, let alone would hear me. I sensed that if
life had any answers, I would find them in God. That conclusion
came to me in a way that my intellect fought, and yet something
within whispered, "That's it."

I offered my first conscious adult prayer that night. A few days
later I obtained a New Testament, started reading, and soon
found myself absorbed in it.

I struggled for nearly a year before I could intellectually grasp
the existence of God. I discovered a loving God who created me
and pronounced me good despite all the experiential evidence to
the contrary. I could look into the dark corners of my life. I could
face the parts of myself I didn't like. I didn't solve all the problems, but at least I started moving in the right direction.

The introspection that comes from loneliness made me think of
nineteenth-century philosopher and theologian Søren Kierke-
gaard. Long before Freud and psychoanalysis, he underwent an
intense process he called reflection—a distinctive inward probing.
He discovered the value of the process as well as its limitations.

The more he got into himself, the more he experienced the
distress that he termed *despair* or *sickness unto death.* He found
only one helpful way out. He called it a leap of faith into the
outstretched hands of God.

That leap of faith doesn't end all the loneliness and despair
either. God's presence brings comfort. When we talk of faith (as
compared to absolute and irrefutable knowing), its very nature

implies doubt. As we leap, we "leap into the dark," and we don't know if the outstretched arms of God will catch us.

Yet God comes through. We discover the truth that "underneath are the everlasting arms" (Deut. 33:27).

5. *Loneliness tells us we are alive.* My own isolation led me to reexamine my priorities and my values. I found that life is a precious gift.

My loneliness keeps me open to new situations, new people, a discovery of new truths or new emphases upon old truths. I recently talked with Bob, a colleague whose wife died three years ago from cancer. They had been married for thirty-one years.

"The image I remember most was coming into an empty and dark house at night," he told me. "It had previously been home, full of the sounds of children and grandchildren. Jane's art students coming and going brought laughter and busyness. But suddenly there was dead silence.

"I sat in the big red chair. I was lonely and quiet. I would have remained there a lot more hours, but I had a strong group of friends who called or visited.

"After the initial stages of grief, I began to feel comforted and comfortable. I no longer needed to run away. I faced my singleness and it made me aware of my loneliness. But one thing sustained me. I knew God had been with me in the past and would not leave me in the future."

When I asked Bob about the positive aspects of his loneliness, he said, "Tension subsided. My life had been too busy and too cluttered in a dozen different ways. I gained a new awareness of my body and my feelings." He also learned the joy of just being alive.

6. *Loneliness can become a friend.* When we keep our lives filled with noise and activity, we have little time to reflect.

When people come home at night, they rush to turn on the TV. When they get inside their cars, they flip on their radios. In most offices people can't work without piped-in music. Can we eat in a restaurant without soft melodies in the background?

When we insist compulsively on noise (music or any other sound), we betray our fear of alienation. We hate the discomfort of being alone with our own thoughts.

When we reflect, we think new thoughts. We see life differently. We learn that we can be alone and still be all right.

One value of accepting loneliness—embracing it as a friend—is that we discover many things about ourselves. And in the discovery, we learn we are lovable.

7. *Loneliness is a joyous/fearsome thing.* Loneliness keeps us uncertain, unable to give definitive and final answers.

"It's how I perceive it today," a friend said. "Tomorrow I may think differently." He didn't vacillate. He merely wanted me to understand his openness.

Loneliness keeps us open to new possibilities, new ideas, and new experiences and can open the door for creative solitude. Being alone with ourselves then becomes an adventure in discovery. We get in touch with ourselves and our humanity. We find ourselves more attuned to the human cries in the world and we want to respond.

8. *Loneliness forces us to think about loving ourselves.* We live in the tension between trusting that we are acceptable and fearing that we're not. Nobody escapes that dilemma. With all of us, it's a matter of degree.

One of Vern's favorite prayers says:

> God, help me believe and trust that loneliness
> and emptiness are part of your loving creation.

This prayer acknowledges the pathos of being less than God. We might change the prayer to read, *Help me to believe that death and suffering are part of your loving creation.*

In my own loneliness I've contemplated who I am and who I want to become as a finished product. In those moments of loneliness I begin to understand the peculiar talents God has given to me. I respond to the call of faithfulness in using those talents.

Without loneliness I would never intentionally walk a path of self-discovery. Loneliness lights up the significant values for me and takes me to the level of my deepest needs.

Someone once told me that loneliness makes us stare at our reflection the same way we gaze at untouched photographs of ourselves. We see our imperfections and warts.

In my loneliness I also view others differently. I am learning to feel more in touch with them when in their presence. I assume that they, too, experience this dreaded aloneness. As I become more comfortable with loneliness as a life's companion, I find more opportunity to reach out to others. I want to enrich their lives as I know they can enrich my own.

10

Knowing Enough

John spent most of his first thirty-five years as a loner. He said, "I thought I could figure anything out by consulting the right source. Every problem revolved around knowledge. People use words, and words carry inexact meanings that confuse. If we want to know, we only have to search for the source and the answer is there."

Although a little extreme, John expressed what many people seem to believe. "If only I knew enough, I could . . ."

Or can we?

Kinds of Knowledge

One kind of knowledge says that if we know enough it will make us happy. If not happy, at least we'll be content. This attitude implies any or all of the following, that

- if we take enough self-help courses
- if we undergo analysis thoroughly enough
- if we work hard enough at knowing ourselves
- and, most importantly, if we know enough about ourselves we'll reach our ultimate goal of happiness in life.

A second kind of knowledge comes from the purveyors of pop psychology. They pound away at the theme, "There is no limit to your ability. There is no mountain you can't climb, no sale you can't make if you have confidence in yourself."

This approach to knowledge pushes us toward maximizing our potential. Unfortunately it may push and promise more than it can provide. As human beings we have an obligation to be all that we can be. But what happens to our no-limit thinking when, no matter how hard we try, we can't pull it off?

Vern observed people like that in the hospital with terminal illnesses who decide to "outthink" their disease.

One physician commented, "Suppose you're wrestling with somebody who is bigger and stronger than you. If you have the right attitude, a lot of confidence in yourself, and focus all your energy on winning, you might overpower the other person. If, however, you are wrestling a five-hundred-pound gorilla, even with all of your energy you would still be pinned down.

"There are limits to what you can do in life. Sometimes those limits make you feel like you're wrestling a five-hundred-pound gorilla." Continuing to wrestle the gorilla can only end in one way—we lose to the animal's greater strength.

A third kind of knowledge holds that if we study hard enough and long enough, we can have what we want. That was my friend John's attitude. But what happens when we seek answers no one can give us? What about situations in which, even if we studied endlessly, we still could not grasp the material?

We need to put forth our best effort. Yet effort alone isn't enough. We need also to recognize that we can't win in every situation no matter how talented, committed, or persevering we are. We keep running into 500-pound gorillas.

A fourth kind of knowledge focuses on learning to communicate clearly. Once we can do that, we can solve all our problems.

One response for troubled marriages today is to offer workshops or seminars on communication skills, to help people clarify their problems. Unfortunately, when some graduates confront conflicts after that, they say, "This is a communication problem."

Their statements suggest that if they could learn how to rephrase their statements and be clearer in expressing what they want, they would have their desires fulfilled, be happy, and move toward solving all their problems.

In learning to communicate more clearly and effectively, we go a long way down the road to solving problems. But such skills are rarely sufficient by themselves. Instead of solving problems, good communication skills merely enable us to express our situations more clearly. We can face the situations and also realize our limitations and the limitations of others.

I could say to my wife, "I want more physical affection." That states my desire clearly.

My wife could answer, "I'm not demonstrative. I don't want to offer any more physical expression than I'm already giving you."

I've made my wants clear and so has she. But we haven't settled anything. We just know more about how the other feels.

Good communication enhances clarity. We can be quite clear and still not get what we want.

A fifth kind of knowledge says that if we learn enough about ourselves, we'll love ourselves. That doesn't work either—not with knowledge alone. We do need to know ourselves better. Part of living involves an innate search for clearer self-understanding.

Reviewing these various kinds of knowledge emphasizes that they are imperfect. They help us understand that we live in an imperfect world. And we, imperfect beings, are part of God's loving creation.

Those words sound simple enough. Yet in practical experience many of us refuse to believe them. I think of Todd, an outstanding businessman who insisted, "There is no deal I can't cut." He only had to know the client better or to figure out shrewder methods or to learn clearer ways of expressing himself. But eventually he could do it.

This attitude made him innovative and tenacious as he kept looking for ways to make his business deals. And Todd's tactics worked. He made big bucks. However, when he carried that attitude over into his home life, all his foolproof methods backfired. He believed he could always get what he wanted from his wife. He just had to try a little harder to discover the right way. Unfortunately, this meant that he actually treated her like an object. He could manipulate her (he used the word *manage*) if he could remember to do and say the right things. He refused to admit that life at home didn't operate the same way as life in business.

In his thinking, she had no ultimate right to say no. If he applied the right kind of pressure with subtlety and stayed with it, she would give in. When she went contrary to his wishes, her defiance became a greater challenge—but one to which he felt equal.

She stopped giving in. She did things he didn't like. "She turned against me," Todd said. Her rebellion enraged him and he refused to accept no for an answer.

After a few months, he started to wonder, What's wrong with me? What am I doing wrong? Why is she treating me like this? He convinced himself that he was doing everything right, which meant she caused their problems. He told her so. After all, common sense said that somebody had to be deficient.

Since Todd could not accept his own inadequacy, he continued to blame his wife. His constant tirades caused her to lose self-confidence. For a long time she accepted his accusations as true. But she didn't give in.

The stress heated up. One day the school authorities recommended they send their son to a counseling program. Todd refused. "Let everyone see how bad he acts and that it comes about because of *your* bad attitude."

Todd had run out of "nice attempts" and was resorting to coercion. He refused to acknowledge that all of us—including himself—run into unsolvable situations. No matter how much we know or what we do, we can't always succeed.

We also need to remember that at times no matter how reasonable or fair our requests and no matter what we do, our needs still don't get met.

If we perceive our lack of cutting a deal as failure, our self-confidence slips. We moan and worry. We ask, "What's wrong with me?"

Todd didn't understand his inability to win every time. Although he is in therapy, he may never understand.

While self-help and support groups and therapy are valuable, our knowledge will still have gaps and blind spots. We never have enough knowledge. If we ignore or deny this, we begin to believe in our own omnipotence (even if we would not use that word). We boast, "I can do anything if I amass enough information and work hard enough."

Paul warned Timothy about the ungodly people who would appear in the last days. He said that they were "always learning but never able to acknowledge the truth" (2 Tim. 3:7, NIV).

Surprisingly, we can do far more than we dreamed possible. We never know until we try. Yet we're on a never-ending climb if we can't accept that sometimes our best tactics and strategies don't work. When they fail, we face the gap between what we want (and possibly deserve) but can't have.

The Dilemma of Knowledge

When knowledge and effort don't produce what we want, we find ourselves facing a dilemma. For those who follow the quest for knowledge and expect achievement, the dilemma is that we are still confronted with helplessness, despite our knowledge.

Albert, now sixty years old, became a millionaire in his forties. Albert was an expert at making money. He's no longer working because, he says, "It's not fun anymore." He had focused on making a fortune. It was as if he said, When I become a millionaire, then I'll be somebody. He made the money and learned that he didn't feel much different about himself. Acquiring possessions never fulfilled his expectation of getting a sense of self-worth.

Albert says, "I feel worthless. I don't know why. Everyone tells me I ought to be the happiest man in the world." He shakes his head uncomprehendingly. "I've got a wonderful wife, three children, and two grandchildren. We all have beautiful homes and cars. But I don't care about the money, the houses, or the things. I don't even care about my own family. What kind of man am I?"

Friends advise him. "Albert, just get busy again." "Albert, you're tired. Relax and enjoy yourself, and you'll soon be able to get back in harness again." Some, not so subtle, have lectured him. "You have everything any man could want. Stop thinking about yourself. Just be grateful!"

All the ideas his friends suggest sound fine. However, they don't help him solve his dilemma. For him, achievement and success have proved dissatisfying. For most of his sixty years Albert concentrated on one thing—making it big. He missed out on other dimensions in his life.

Albert has been going to therapy for almost a year. He is making progress, but I wonder if he will finally learn that his sense of self-esteem was tied in with his productivity. When succeeding lost its allure, it left him with a vague sense of being of no value.

When we link our self-esteem to success we're in danger. Failure, regardless of how we define it, happens to all of us. Failures jeopardize that fragile self-esteem. Consider two significant kinds:

First, *real failure:* "If we had worked harder or longer, it would have been successful."

When we view real failure for what it is, we can evaluate life more honestly. "I fell short. I got discouraged. I needed to work harder. Next time I'll know better."

Or we can say, "I did my best. It didn't work, that's all. Maybe it will work next time."

Second, *irrational failure:* No matter what we might have done, we had no control over the situation. It would have happened anyway. The economy hit bottom. A better product came along or one that a company could market cheaper.

Failure can be helpful. It can teach us that, even though our work failed or our dreams died, we are still lovable creatures. We must remind ourselves that God created us to have value for *being,* not for *doing.*

We can learn better from failure if we begin to grasp that we need such experiences for us to grow. Every human being fails. Our inability to achieve through sheer willpower, intention, persistence, and hard work is part of being human. To fail does not make us less valuable.

Vern used to have a sign in his office that read:

> Good judgment comes from experience;
> experience comes from bad judgment.

Part of life's true education is for us to grasp that we can and will make mistakes. But we can learn from them. If our parents hadn't allowed us to fall, we would never have learned to walk. We must make mistakes in order to grow.

The Failed Knowledge Question

When we believe that if we know enough we won't make mistakes, that leads us to insist that we *must* not make mistakes.

Then when we fail—and we all do—what happens? Reality confronts us and sometimes immobilizes us. Once immobilized, we feel badly because we failed, and then we feel badly because, even though we know the answers to all the questions, we're still immobilized. Being immobilized means not being productive. When we measure our worth by productivity or success, a question haunts us: What happens when knowing enough isn't enough? Who am I when I'm neither successful nor productive? Am I then nobody?

We find it hard enough to deal with not knowing enough, of not making the grade, and not being productive enough. We find it even more painful when our lack challenges our personhood. It hurts to lose. Then failing becomes equal to being worthless. These experiences add up to make us think that we're inadequate, unacceptable to others and (more important) to ourselves.

For example, some men think that by showing their wives more attention, being more affectionate, sensitizing themselves to their needs, they themselves will feel more adequate. Being sensitive and responsive to our spouses is an important part of loving. Therefore, some think that if we learn the mechanics of being more loving and tender, more caring and supportive, we can make ourselves more acceptable and our partners happier (or more manageable?). But what happens to all that knowledge and deep understanding on days when we wake up in a grumpy mood? When we feel too tired to give our mates any attention? When our spouses want more than we can give? We learned how to behave and to react. Unfortunately, much of the technique or strategy that we learned never became an inner part of ourselves.

These inabilities to achieve our goals wound our self-esteem. Sometimes we persist in trying and still don't get everything we want. Finally we wonder, Did I miss some information or vital fact? Could I have given more? Did I not give enough?

Being loved, being valuable, being worthwhile is not dependent upon a knowledge of behavioral and psychological principles. Fundamental heartfelt knowledge is bedrock to our ability to accept ourselves when we can't be sensitive and responsive and to accept others when they can't be sensitive and responsive.

We can overcome such an attitude that more knowledge will make us successful only with the belief that we're already lovable.

We give out of gratitude, not in order to get something in return. To give with expectations of return is bargaining. It's a transaction. There is nothing wrong with bargaining, but don't call it love.

From Knowledge to Change

We can continue in our quest for knowledge with the idea that our knowledge will lead us to change. Knowledge can do so, but we have no guarantee. We make radical changes only (1) when we hurt too badly to continue doing things the same way as before or (2) when we realize that our way of coping (handling/manipulating) stops working.

Our coping methods stop for any number of reasons:

- We have changed externally
- Conditions are no longer the same
- Our business associates or spouses no longer respond to us as they once did
- A teen leaves home
- A death occurs in the family
- A baby is born
- We experience the male mid-life crisis or the female menopause
- Our health deteriorates

Todd, the businessman mentioned earlier, will constantly find it a temptation to cut a deal with the people, no matter how much he changes. He'll struggle with the temptation to get what he wants by offering enducements.

The Chinese symbol for crisis means a *dangerous opportunity.* In crisis, we know we must do something. We cannot continue as before. Todd's actions show he chose destructive behavior. He blamed. He would not adapt to his family's needs.

Previously Todd sent flowers when his wife wasn't happy with something he did. The gift changed her mood. Eventually she saw that he was trying to buy her acquiescence. Her new rejection created anger in him.

Albert's pattern of earning money worked for him for at least forty years and made him a millionaire. But it doesn't work now. If Albert had died at age forty-nine, he would never have had to face his dilemma. He didn't die. He may have another twenty years. What will he do with the rest of his life? No one knows. He's in a lot of pain. He's afraid. Yet he also grudgingly admits he has the opportunity to discover something new. It remains to be seen whether he'll learn to value himself.

One liability with knowledge is that we understand more than we can put into practice. One of Vern's favorite aphorisms says:

> No strength is not also a liability.
> No liability is not also a strength.

Yet when we try to decide what is a strength and what is a liability, we are determining what makes us valuable. Usually we think of intelligence, knowledge, and education as strengths. These can also function as liabilities, when, for example, we grasp ideas and concepts intellectually but our feelings haven't caught up.

Ray has been unhappy in his marriage for years. He has been trying to change his wife into what he believes she ought to be. It hasn't worked. He has considered divorce hundreds of times. Intellectually he grasps that leaving Marie won't solve all his problems. He also realizes that continuing his pattern of behavior hurts him and her.

Yet his neediness and hurt-little-boy feelings get in the way and prevent his acting on this knowledge. Ray faces the gap between what he knows to be right and what he's able to do at this time. He tends to be unaccepting of his own self as he works toward being less controlling.

Ray needs to accept that he's moving slower than he wants to but that another part of his nature makes him cautious. Unless he can understand these characteristics, he's constantly going to be self-critical. His self-criticism alone won't lead to growth. It may convolute pain that prevents his doing anything constructive.

Or consider a baby's learning to walk. Little Nora had to fall many times. One of the early things Nora will learn (if she's like most children) is to land on her padded rear end and not on her nose. If Nora's parents refuse to let her fall, she won't learn to walk. She has to feel what it's like to be off balance before she can know how to balance herself.

This problem of knowledge presents nothing new to us. We humans have always struggled with it. Paul knew all the right ways and exactly what God expected (see Rom. 7:14–25). Yet he said that he kept doing the opposite. He finally cried out, "Wretched man that I am! Who will deliver me from this body of death?"

Although Paul answered his own questions by turning to God's grace, he never said that it solved everything. He learned to forgive himself for failing. He realized that he didn't have to live under a cloud of condemnation and criticism.

True Knowledge

In the early church, a group known as the Gnostics (from the Greek word for knowledge) rose to prominence. They fiercely contended that true knowledge—a kind of superior, esoteric understanding acquired through diligent effort—makes us true Christians. They insisted that proper knowledge led to correct behavior, which led to God. The majority of church leaders denounced this as heresy. (The book of 1 John is essentially a discourse against Gnosticism.) We base our faith, the church leaders declared, in God's grace. Knowledge—of any kind— doesn't save us. In effect, they said, "Our heads can get in the way of our hearts. We understand more than we live. We often know what to do and how to do it without having the power to perform. We must turn to God for that help."

Ideally, we never stop trying to know ourselves. Part of the good knowledge we acquire involves ourselves more fully. We accept our good side and the shadow side of our personality. We don't stop even there.

Self-knowledge that leads to self-love says we appreciate the shadow side of our good qualities and the sunny side of our weaknesses. We accept our wholeness and discover within ourselves strength and weakness, gain and loss. We also learn we have the ability to make choices and the power to change.

Once we realize that

- knowing more doesn't make us better and
- not knowing doesn't make us less valuable

we begin to grasp the proper place of knowledge in our lives—to lead us to a greater sense of who we are and to value ourselves highly.

The best kind of knowledge says, "I *know* I am loved and I love myself."

Appendix A
Taking Responsibility for Our Lives

Here is an exercise that will help you look at how you are spending your life in light of how you would like to spend your life. When you have completed this exercise, you can begin to take responsibility for making the changes necessary to change your life to what you want it to be.

On a sheet of paper, make three columns, the center one being the widest. Divide your day into approximately one-hour intervals and list your activities in each period of time. (See the sample on the next page.)

An alternative to a daily schedule would be a weekly description of your principal activities and the amount of time you devote to each.

In the sample, the activities are in broad categories. Please be more specific in your list to show how you actually spend your day.

7 A.M.	Awaken, get ready for the day, breakfast	
8	Leave for work	
9–12	Work (describe specific tasks)	
12–1 P.M.	Lunch period	
1–4	Work	
5	Return home	
5–6	Yard work	
6	Evening meal, listen to evening news	
7–11	Watch television	
11	Go to bed	

Once you have completed your 24-hour day, in the right column mark each of these activities in one of three ways:

E Activities I particularly enjoy
N Those I would rather not do or dislike doing
T Activities I tolerate, but about which I have no strong feeling

Part of your list might now look like this:

| 8 | Leave for work | T |
| 9–12 | Work | E |

Once you have filled out the right column, answer these questions.

1. What do these answers tell you about how you spend your day?

2. Express how you feel about the way you spend your time.

3. What roles do you fulfill during this 24-hour period?

4. Look over the roles you have listed. Are these the roles you want to fulfill in your life? Give reasons for your answer.

Repeat the entire exercise, but instead of writing how you *actually* spend your time, write how you would *like* to spend it—the ideal arrangement.

What are the major differences between the way you actually spend your time and the way you wish you had spent your time?

Appendix B
Making Ourselves Better

Don't we all want to be better? Most of us have some sense that we can make ourselves into individuals with deeper levels of kindness, understanding, helpfulness, intimacy, or whatever qualities we desire.

Unfortunately we can't *make* ourselves into anything. We can do things that assist in our journey toward becoming more of the kind of person we want to be. If we insist on making or remaking ourselves, we miss the entire point of being lovable simply by being alive and part of God's creation.

Here are six practical exercises to help you learn to like yourself better. None of these suggestions will *give* you a love for yourself. These are practical tips to reinforce your self-esteem.

1. Accurate self-assessment

We can take a battery of tests from clinical psychologists, learning centers, and colleges. We need to go beyond checking on our IQ, which gives us only a partial assessment.

In the New Testament, Paul writes about spiritual gifts in 1 Corinthians 12, Romans 12, and Ephesians 4. While these lists don't exhaust the talents God gives people, they are good places to begin.

In recent years several Christian groups have come up with spiritual-gifts inventories. The most obvious method for identifying these gifts involves asking one's friends or co-workers in church projects to list the gifts they observe.

An example springs to mind of Susan, the Sunday school superintendent of the church I once served as pastor. In a small-group setting we talked with her about the gifts we recognized. One of the people said, "You're a terrific administrator."

"Me?" She immediately started to dismiss it.

Others spoke up. All of us confirmed her gift, even though we had not thought much about it previously. Susan never had considered her gift as any kind of special ability.

We all have areas in which we consider ourselves defective when we are not. Carl Jung referred to this as our "shadow" side. We need appreciation for those qualities. The outside confirmation encourages us to accept and to develop these talents.

Alfred Adler devised a theory called "compensation for organ inferiority." He believed that when people have a "real deficit," they have a tendency either to deny it or to overcompensate.

For example, during my time in graduate school, I knew a woman student with thin blond hair. One day she bought a hairpiece and had it dyed to match her natural color. That large hairpiece made her small head look topheavy. That's overcompensation.

Adler said we sometimes displace these deficits into other parts of ourselves. A man may be quite ugly but bright. He displaces his unattractiveness by calling himself stupid.

If we have real deficits that we can't change, most of us learn to ignore them or compensate in other areas, such as the awkward boy who fails in sports but concentrates on being a brilliant student.

Sometimes we try to make up for it with what one theorist called "a narcissistic extension," like the short actor Mickey Rooney, who has had seven wives all taller than himself.

Besides the need for an accurate self-assessment through outside sources, we also need to find appreciation and value for the positives in our lives.

2. Journal keeping

Journal keeping has proven helpful to many people. I kept a daily journal from mid-1972 through mid-1986. That exercise taught me a great deal about myself.

My reflective journal, as I called it, contained not just the events of the day, like a diary, but also a record of my impressions and feelings. I acknowledged my anxieties, fears, hopes, and ambitions. I became more familiar with this creature named Cec Murphey. I strove for rigorous honesty with myself and wrote the journal only for my own use.

Over the course of years my weaknesses stared glaringly at me from the page. Often I stopped typing to pray for God's help. But I also began to recognize areas of strength that I had never noticed before. In the summer of 1986 I abandoned my reflective journal. For me the process had become too analytical. I wanted to try other approaches.

Local colleges and churches offer courses in journal keeping. There is a plethora of books about what the authors call "creative journal keeping." Many of them are in large workbook sizes. They usually rely on some form of imagery.

The first such workbook I went through asked me to imagine going to a castle (Christopher Biddle, *The Castle of the Pearl;* New York: Harper & Row, 1983). Once inside, I presided at a banquet. The instructions told me to invite nine people (living or dead) to share my banquet. I was to write down their names hurriedly, not asking myself why. I looked over my list. My heart had chosen quite a different list from what my rational nature would have selected.

The next instruction asked me to talk to each of those nine people. I was to say anything I wanted to. It surprised me that I had written down the name of my younger brother, Mel, who had died three years earlier. As I pondered what to say to him, I realized how deeply I loved him. We had squabbled in hundreds of ways during childhood in a kind of love-hate relationship. Yet in the last months of his life, knowing his terminal condition, he phoned me long distance regularly. "You're the only one who understands me, Cec," he said once. Now a lot of stored-up grief came to the surface, and I mourned my loss far more than I had at the time of his death.

As I moved on through the journal for the next six weeks, the exercises pushed me to look at my family and my relationships with other people. It also provided several ways for me to examine myself more closely with a loving, affirmative approach. I had a greater self-appreciation by the time I finished.

Devotees of creative journal keeping claim that the habit helps us to

- express deep-seated feelings and inner thoughts
- sort out seemingly random experiences in our lives
- make more conscious choices
- define and implement changes
- enrich our relationship with ourselves and others
- find a deeper meaning to life.

Although creative journal keepers start with specific exercises, they encourage readers to modify or expand the instructions, invent their own ways, or find new means of spontaneous self-expression.

3. Self-Talk

Nothing has helped me more in my quest for learning to love myself than the discovery of self-talk. Some call it by other terms, such as autosuggestion, autogenics, and self-programming. The idea comes from a simple premise: that we talk to ourselves all the time. In fact, we can't *not* talk to ourselves. That's part of being human, of having the power of self-consciousness.

What we tell ourselves is manifest in how we feel about ourselves. If we fill our minds with negative input, we get a negative outflow. Henry Ford once said something like, "If you think you will succeed or if you think you will fail, you are right."

How many of us say these things about ourselves (and sometimes out loud, which makes their imprint even stronger)?

"I'm such a klutz."
"I'm the world's worst at remembering names."
"I'm no good with figures."
"I always blow it when I take a test."
"I can't do anything right today."

Much of how we feel about ourselves depends on what we have heard others say about us. I have read that our self-image becomes fairly fixed by age seven but that we can change or modify it. That modifying takes work and dedication.

Whether being "fairly fixed" is fact or not, I do know that when we're young we have no way to discriminate between true and false information we receive about ourselves.

For instance, my father used to call me lazy. It usually happened when he assigned chores to me and my two younger brothers. The middle brother, Mel, seldom did his work. I wasted a lot of energy trying to get him to work and finally did the chores myself, or the work didn't get done. Then came Dad's verbal assault.

I grew up believing I was lazy. As an adult I saw physical tiredness as a sign of weakness. I kept pushing myself to do more things in less time. I grew up as an overachiever, always trying to prove to my dad that I was not a lazy person.

I am not lazy, but I accepted that word as an accurate description. Oddly enough, through the years people have remarked on my high energy level and the rapidity with which I get things done.

I have used the self-talk concept to help me realize the truth about my energy and activity level. I have also devised two exercises to aid in developing a more honest and positive self-view.

Self-Editing. From today onward, listen to the words that come from your own lips. Don't allow yourself to say negative things about you. If such things slip out, correct them immediately.

Here's an example of how it worked with me. My friend Jerry helped me shop for a new car. He likes doing it and I've always hated dealing with salespeople. When we talked with the sellers, Jerry asked the questions and I listened. It turned out to be a great experience. I liked the car I bought and appreciated the deal Jerry helped me to make.

In telling friends about my adventure, I said, "I'm not much of a businessman so I asked Jerry to help." I realized immediately what I had said. "No, that's not true," I corrected. "I *am* a good businessman. Because I don't like to bargain, I asked a friend to do that part for me. Isn't being a good businessman knowing where to go for help?"

Help your friends avoid self-putdowns. Listen to what they say about themselves. This not only helps them but keeps you sensitive to the words going on inside your own head.

In my support group when one person said something like, "I'm such a jerk," I would interrupt with, "Please don't say that about yourself. You are not a jerk. You may have done something dumb, but you're no jerk."

As simple as that seems, after a few weeks the others caught on. We refused to make derogatory statements about ourselves. This pact presented a little problem at first because men don't usually know how to affirm one another. We do it with what I call the backslap compliment. We laughingly insult our close friends as a sign of our affection.

By diligent attention we have all learned how to express affection or appreciation by saying it straight. We can now say "I like you" or "You are a special friend."

Self-Talk Statements. On a 3×5 card write three self-affirming statements about yourself as described below. You don't have to believe them, but they are statements you would like to be true, such as "I love myself." Write the statements

- concisely, using no more than ten words
- positively
- in the present tense as if they have already been accomplished

1. Write a statement about loving yourself. *I love myself.* Use *like* if that's more comfortable.

2. Write a statement referring to some aspect of commitment to God. If you are following the exercise Vern suggested in chapter 5, "The Divine Option," your sentence might be: *Each day I pray for ——— minutes.* (Don't worry if you have already missed three days of praying. It's the habit you want to establish.)

3. Write a statement about an area in your life that troubles you. One man who did this exercise struggled with holding grudges. His statement read, *I let go of anger.*

If you do this exercise alone, you do all three parts of it. Or two trusted friends can help you.

Read your first statement: "I love myself."

Read it again but in the second person with your own name: "Cec, you love yourself."

Read it a third time using the third person and your own name: "Cec loves himself."

Go through each of the statements that way. Do it several times each day, every day, for at least three weeks. (It takes a minimum of three weeks to establish any new habit.)

The experts in self-talk techniques advise repeating the statements to yourself aloud, with as much enthusiasm as possible, a minimum of six times a day.

After a few days or weeks, you might want to add additional statements. I have a list of thirty statements I make to myself ten times daily when I run. I have discovered that they keep my mind positive toward myself and also help me in viewing my world more optimistically.

4. Accepting approval

Abraham Maslow taught that we establish self-esteem by receiving approval and respect from others. If I interpret him correctly, he meant that while we already have innate value, we *perceive* it largely through the affirmations of other people.

In a similar vein, Harry Stack Sullivan stressed that we learn and enlarge our self-concepts by the "reflected appraisals" of the significant people in our lives.

Structured exercises at retreats and workshops can aid individuals in receiving significant approval from others. In my own support group, we spent half an hour one night in genuinely affirming and appreciating one another.

We did it in the simplest form possible. The person who started turned to the man on his right and said something direct like, "You are easy to talk to."

The receiver could make only one response: "Thank you."

Then that person made an affirming statement to the person on *his* right, and so on around the six-man group. We went around a second time, turning to the person on our left.

Another time we selected one man to be the first receiver and the five of us said true and appreciative things about him. The next man then became the receiver and so on, until all of us had had a turn.

As a variation, one night in our support group John talked about the rough ordeal he had been going through. It included financial pressures, the death of a close relative, and troubles with his younger son.

Jerry said, "John, tell me something positive about you. What do you like about yourself?"

John hesitated and the rest of us insisted that he answer.

"Well," he said hesitantly, "I'm a good father. I'm not—"

"No negatives," I said. "You're a good father. What else?"

"I'm interested in other people."

Five men nodded or verbally agreed. Item by item John mentioned other positive things about himself.

"That's not all," Jerry said. "Think a little more about it."

Within ten minutes, John had given us a long list of positive things about himself.

As I listened, I watched John's facial expression change. He had started with a downcast set about his eyes and mouth. By the time he stopped, he didn't glow, but his eyes had come alive, as if saying, I'm really better than I thought.

We didn't give John value. We allowed him to recognize positive qualities about himself.

5. Prayer

Here are three prayers that many have found helpful in their search to appreciate themselves. Put the first two in a prominent place like the bathroom mirror where you will see them every day.

My favorite prayer goes like this:

Loving God, show me the truth about myself no matter how beautiful it may be.

My special prayer:

I thank you for making me a unique, unrepeatable miracle of God.

My Woody prayer requires a brief explanation. Woody is one of those special gems whom God occasionally sends into our lives. Although a man of little formal education, he has provided me with jewels of wisdom throughout our eight years of association.

One day Woody said, "You know, I used to feel selfish about praying for myself. I kept thinking that I ought to forget about me and concentrate on interceding for others. Then it hit me that if I were somebody else, I wouldn't hesitate to pray for me."

He told me that he had started praying for himself daily in the third person, by stepping back and looking at himself as a caring outsider would. He prayed something like this:

God, Woody wants to love himself. He keeps seeing all his failures and his shortcomings. Won't you help him get beyond that? Let him see that you love him, no matter how often he fails.

6. The Bible

Many people follow a daily systematic study of the Bible. Selecting a few verses for meditating or memorizing is also helpful.

Copy each verse you want to use on a 3×5 file card. Read the verse over several times. Think about what you're reading. Ask God to help you understand the message you need. Here are some sample verses:

For God so loved the world that he gave his only Son, that whoever believes in him should not perish but have eternal life.
—John 3:16

I have created you and cared for you since you were born. I will be your God through all your lifetime, yes, even when your hair is white with age. I made you and I will care for you. I will carry you along and be your Savior.
—Isaiah 46:3–4, TLB

Then God said, "Let us make man in our image, after our likeness; and let them have dominion over the fish of the sea, and over the birds of the air, and over the cattle, and over all the earth, and over every creeping thing that creeps upon the earth." . . . And God saw everything that he had made, and behold, it was very good.
—Genesis 1:26, 31

We love, because he first loved us.
—1 John 4:19

Fear not, for I am with you. Do not be dismayed. I am your God. I will strengthen you; I will help you; I will uphold you with my victorious right hand.
—Isaiah 41:10, TLB

Because the Lord is my Shepherd, I have everything I need!
—Psalm 23:1, TLB

We know how dearly God loves us, and we feel this warm love everywhere within us because God has given us the Holy Spirit to fill our hearts with his love.

—Romans 5:5, TLB

Are not two sparrows sold for a penny? And not one of them will fall to the ground without your Father's will. But even the hairs of your head are all numbered. Fear not, therefore; you are of more value than many sparrows.

—Matthew 10:29–31

I have loved you with an everlasting love.

—Jeremiah 31:3

Appendix C
My Lifeline

On a sheet of paper, draw a horizontal line across the width of the paper. On the left side, write your birth year. How long do you reasonably expect to live? Consider that for a moment and then, on the right end of the line, write that year. Write the current year at the approximate place you are now.

Your lifeline might look like this:

— — — — — — — — — — — — — — — —

| 1940 | 1988 | 2010 |

Study that line for a few minutes by asking yourself these questions:

> How many years have I already lived?
> How many years do I expect to have left?
> On the whole, am I pleased with what I've done with my life?
> If I died tomorrow, could I say, "This has been enough"?
> How do I want to spend the rest of my life?

This exercise of Vern's puts a spatial, visual limit on life. None of us lives forever. You are now looking at life with its limitations. As you move closer to the right side of the paper, you have fewer choices left. You become more aware of the shortness of time. You start facing the reality that you can no longer do everything you want in life.

One man who did this exercise had been toying with a career

change for months. This exercise helped him to make the decision to change jobs. Another said it "evoked a tremendous sense of urgency to make the rest of life more meaningful and not just to fritter it away."

Appendix D
Life Values

Because this exercise of Vern's evokes strong feelings, you may want to do it with some friends or use it in a support group of which you are a member. You and the others will then be able to discuss your reactions to it.

For the exercise to be effective, you will need to think of the most important things in your life. Then, on each of five sheets of paper, write one word or phrase.

On the first paper, answer this question: *What is my favorite possession?* Make your answer a tangible and inanimate object. It could be a house, a photograph, a piece of jewelry, or a car.

On the second page of paper write, *What physical activity do I enjoy most?* List an activity that requires the use of your body. Examples could be gardening, sexual activity, playing tennis, or reading.

On the third page of paper, write, *What possible but as yet unfulfilled dream do I have?* This is something you want to do and can achieve if you work hard and apply yourself. This dream could be anything from getting married, having a child, seeing your last child leave home, or owning your own business to going on a Hawaiian vacation to building a model airplane.

On pages four and five you will be writing the name of a person. While you might think of the same person for both, for this exercise use different individuals.

On page four write, *Who is the most important person in my life with whom I have unfinished business?* This significant person is the one to whom you need to say things as yet unsaid. The unfinished business can be as simple as "I love you" or "I hate you" or "If you do that one more time—" or "Please forgive me for—" or "I forgive you for—" or "You have never once thanked me for—."

Fifth, and probably the easiest category for most: *Who is the person I love most and who loves me?*

When you have completed the responses on each of the five pieces of paper, the words you have written are a kind of shorthand list of the most important aspects of your life. Take a few minutes to read each item and recall how that person, thing, or dream gained importance for you. Reflect how this list summarizes your personal history.

You do not have to write anything more. Do the rest of this exercise in complete silence. Pay attention to any physical responses you have as well as emotional reactions, if any.

Read this story and follow the directions given in italics.

You have not been feeling well for several weeks. There is nothing you can put your finger on, but you feel tired, worn out. You have to force yourself to get anything done. You had the flu a few weeks earlier so you attribute your present situation to its aftereffects, along with your busy work schedule. You decide you are just making a slow recovery.

The worn-out feelings don't go away. You start waking up in the middle of the night sweating. It concerns you enough that you finally go to a physician. In the course of routine lab work and physical examination, your doctor asks you to sit down with her in her office.

The physician tells you something completely unexpected. You have a disease called AML—acute myelogenous leukemia. (The treatment and prognosis of AML have changed recently. For purposes of this exercise, consider the following to be standard.)

Before you ask your first question, your life has drastically changed. This shocking news requires you to give up something in your life.

Look through your five pieces of paper. Choose one and crumple it. Get rid of it. Whatever you've given up is gone forever; you can never have it back.

You are a curious person, and you want to find out about this disease. You start asking questions. Your physician tells you that in adults this disease is considered controllable but not often curable.

"What does controllable mean?" you ask.

"Controllable means that if you respond to treatment, your life expectancy will increase."

"How long?" you ask. The words stick in your throat.

"Statistically," your doctor says, "you could expect another year and a half to two years."

While you try to absorb that information, you also learn that your treatment requires intensive chemotherapy. You will undergo cycles of treatment at three-week intervals at the hospital. This medicine destroys all fast-growing cells and has side effects such as the loss of your hair. The medicine will irritate your gastrointestinal tract. Your white blood cell count will decrease, and that exposes you to the probability of getting an infection.

As long as you respond to treatment, you will have enough antibiotics and professional care to get you through these infections. Treatment also means that you'll be hospitalized from four to ten weeks, depending on how many cycles of therapy you need to go into remission. You also hear the good news that over 70 percent of the patients go into remission their first time.

You choose treatment, knowing all the facts. You enter the hospital and take your chemotherapy. You stay there for seventy-three days. Your life has changed again. For you, change means loss. You must give up something else in your life.

Choose a second piece of paper, crumple it, and get rid of it.

You have now been home for a week. The chemotherapy was rough on you—you couldn't imagine you would feel so nauseated—but you are in remission. By all medical indicators you are free of disease. You can return to your normal activities, except that you still have not regained your strength and your hair has not grown back.

You return to the hospital's outpatient clinic regularly for more therapy. Except for the inconvenience, you can live your life as you wish. You return to your previous life-style. Yet you live with the troubled thought that statistics say you will relapse within the next year.

With this threat dangling over your head, your recovered health brings a loss. You must give up something else.

Select a third sheet of paper and crumple it up.

It is fourteen months after your initial diagnosis. You have been an exceptional patient. You arranged vacations around your clinic visits. You went to the clinic whenever you had the first symptom. You followed directions completely.

Now you're feeling worn out again, experiencing the same symptoms you had originally. You wake up at night sweating. You're worried about a relapse. You go back to the physician, and she confirms your worst fears.

You have relapsed. You face the certainty that if you do not undergo further treatment the disease will follow its natural course and kill you. Even if you take treatment, your chances of going into remission will be less than 50 percent. This time your decision is much harder.

You choose treatment but ask for a couple of days to get your life in order. You realize that you may never leave the hospital. This realization requires that you give up something else.

Choose a fourth sheet of paper, crumple it, and put it away.

Six weeks into your hospitalization you have a bone marrow test. This is done by boring a small hole in a bone and taking a sample of the marrow to determine if leukemic cells remain. You're waiting for those results.

This is an important test for you. You're miserable. You're running a 104-degree temperature, and your mouth is ulcerated. You have trouble swallowing, you're nauseated, and you have chills. Despite all this, your mind is alert.

Your physician comes to your room. She does something she's never done before; she sits on the side of your bed, takes your hand, looks at you, and says, "I'm sorry."

With that piece of news you must give up the last thing that's important in your life.

Take your last piece of paper and crumple it.

Everything in life that you value is gone. You have died.

Pause for a few minutes and reflect on your experience before reading on.

Even though this is only an exercise, it has an uncanny ability to reproduce the sequence of losses that people go through in life. We slowly lose the things that matter most.

The exercise emphasizes the distinction between the *process* of dying and the *act* of dying. Most people fear the process more than actual death. Death becomes an inexorable sequence of losses over which we have no control. This exercise helps us acknowledge that as we age we lose or give up the things and people important to us.

As we become aware of the process of loss, we are even more aware of what we value most in life. We cast off the other things that, while meaningful, helpful, or significant, are not the most important. Many things to which we attach great value have little real meaning when we view them in light of our total life.

If we live long enough, most of us will become helpless. We face the question, Who are we when we can't do anything?

For example, we tend to define ourselves by our activities. When doing this exercise, we are confronted with great emotional pain. We struggle with life's significant questions, such as, Who am I now that I can't even go to the bathroom without assistance?

The aging process is also the dying process. The dying process takes away our ability to make love, to be productive at work, to be companions. While this varies with individuals, these things are taken from us and we have little choice and often no choice at all. Then we confront the question, Who am I now? Am I of any value in the face of these overwhelming losses? Do I matter? Is life worthwhile?

Dying confronts us with losses in a way that might be likened to being beaten up. The first loss hits us like a strong punch in the stomach. We feel the pain. Then we get hit again. Again. And again. Finally, all we feel is pain and we can no longer think of the separate blows.

In the course of our lives, we need to learn to accept our mortality, our being less than God, the fact that we actually own nothing in our lives. The idea of accepting death requires dealing with limitations and losses and discovering self-values apart from our productivity.

A final but significant point: We do not say that our productivity has no value. We want to say that what we *do* is not what determines our value.